T0317361

Teaching
African Literature Today
29

Editor: Ernest N. Emenyonu
Department of Africana Studies,
University of Michigan-Flint
303 East Kearsley Street, Flint, MI 48502, USA

Deputy Editor: Nana Wilson-Tagoe
Department of Black Studies, University of Missouri,
Kansas City, MO 64110, USA

Assistant Editor: Patricia T. Emenyonu
Department of English, University of Michigan-Flint

Associate Editors: Jane Bryce
Department of Language, Linguistics and Literature
University of West Indies, Cave Hill, Barbados

Maureen N. Eke
Department of English, Central Michigan University
Mount Pleasant, MI 48859, USA

Stephanie Newell
School of English, University of Sussex
Falmer, Brighton BN1 9QN, East Sussex

Charles E. Nnolim
Department of English, School of Humanities
University of Port Harcourt, Rivers State, Nigeria

Ato Quayson
Centre for Diaspora & Transitional Studies,
Room 202, Medical Arts Bldg, 170 St George Street,
Toronto, Ontario, Canada, M5R 2M8

Kwawisi Tekpetey
Department of Humanities, Central State University,
PO Box 1004, Wilberforce, OH 45384, USA

Iniobong I. Uko
Department of English, University of Uyo,
Uyo, Akwa Ibom State, Nigeria

Reviews Editor: James Gibbs
8 Victoria Square, Bristol BS8 4ET, UK
jamesgibbs@btinternet.com

African Literature Today

1-14 were published from London by Heinemann Educational Books and from New York by Africana Publishing Company

*Backlist titles available in the US and Canada from Africa World Press
and in the rest of the world from James Currey, an imprint of Boydell and Brewer*

Note from the publisher on new and forthcoming titles

James Currey Publishers have now joined Boydell & Brewer Ltd.
African Literature Today will continue to be published as an annual volume under the James Currey imprint. North and South American distribution will be available from The University of Rochester Press, 68 Mount Hope Avenue, Rochester, NY 14620-2731, USA, while UK and International distribution will be handled by Boydell & Brewer Ltd., PO Box 9, Woodbridge IP12 3DF, UK.

Call for papers

ALT 30 Reflections & Retrospectives in African Literature Today
(Guest editor: Chimalum Nwankwo; e-mail: muonisi@yahoo.com)

This special issue will be devoted to the memory of some leading voices of African Literature in the twentieth century: Bessie Head, Cyprian Ekwensi, Dennis Brutus, Es'kia Mphahlele, Flora Nwapa and T.M. Aluko. The Editor invites scholars to submit original, previously unpublished articles on any of the authors listed above. Essays can focus on particular work/s, contributions of the chosen writer to the development of African Literature, his/her legacies as an African writer. Essays on critical receptions of a chosen writer's *oeuvre*, or particular works are also welcome.

Guidelines for Submission of Articles

The Editor invites submission of articles or proposals for articles on the announced themes of forthcoming issues:

Ernest N. Emenyonu, *African Literature Today*
Department of Africana Studies, University of Michigan-Flint
303 East Kearsley Street, Flint MI 48502, USA
email: africanliteraturetoday@umflint.edu
Fax: 001 810 766 6719

Submissions will be acknowledged promptly and decisions communicated within six months of the receipt of the paper. Your name and institutional affiliation (with full mailing address and email) should appear on a separate sheet, plus a brief biographical profile of not more than six lines. The editor cannot undertake to return material submitted and contributors are advised to keep a copy of all material sent. Please note that all articles outside the announced themes cannot be considered or acknowledged and that articles should not be submitted via email. Articles should be submitted in the English language.

Length: articles should not exceed 5,000 words

Format: two hard copies plus disk of all articles should be submitted, double-spaced, on one side only of A4 paper, with pages numbered consecutively. Disks may be formatted for PC or AppleMac but please label all files and disks clearly, and save files as Word for Windows or Word for Macintosh.

Style: UK or US spellings, but be consistent. Direct quotations should retain the spelling used in the original source. Check the accuracy of your citations and always give the source, date, and page number in the text and a full reference in the Works Cited at the end of the article. Italicise titles of books or plays. Use single inverted commas throughout except for quotes within quotes which are double. Avoid subtitles or subsection headings within the text.

References: to follow series style (Surname date: page number) in brackets in text. All references/works cited should be listed in full at the end of each article, in the following style:
Surname, name/initial. *title of work*. place, publisher, date
Surname, name/initial. 'title of article'. In surname, name/initial (ed.)
title of work. place of publication, publisher, date
or Surname, name/initial, 'title of article', *Journal*, vol. no.: page no.

Copyright: it is the responsibility of contributors to clear permissions

Reviewers should provide full bibliographic details, including the extent, ISBN and price, and submit to the reviews editor
James Gibbs, 8 Victoria Square, Bristol BS8 4ET, UK
jamesgibbs@btinternet.com

Teaching
African Literature Today
29

A Review

Editor: Ernest N. Emenyonu
Deputy Editor: Nana Wilson-Tagoe
Assistant Editor: Patricia T. Emenyonu

Associate Editors: Jane Bryce
                      Maureen N. Eke
                      Stephanie Newell
                      Charles E. Nnolim
                      Ato Quayson
                      Kwawisi Tekpetey
                      Iniobong I. Uko

Reviews Editor: James Gibbs

JAMES CURREY

HEBN

James Currey
is an imprint of Boydell & Brewer Ltd
PO Box 9, Woodbridge, Suffolk, IP12 3DF, UK

and of

Boydell & Brewer Inc.
668 Mt Hope Avenue, Rochester, NY 14620, USA
www.boydellandbrewer.com
www.jamescurrey.com

HEBN Publishers Plc
1 Ighodaro Rd, Jericho
P.M.B. 5205, Ibadan, Nigeria
www.hebnpublishers.com

1 2 3 4 5 13 12 11

British Library Cataloguing in Publication Data
Teaching African literature today. -- (African literature
    today ; 29)
    1. African literature--Study and teaching (Higher)
    I. Series II. Emenyonu, Ernest, 1939-
    809.8'8'96'00711-dc23

ISBN 978-1-84701-511-2 (James Currey paper)
ISBN 978-978-081-4175 (HEBN paper)

The publisher has no responsibility for the continued existence or accuracy of
URLs for external or third-party internet websites referred to in this book, and
does not guarantee that any content on such websites is, or will remain, accurate
or appropriate.

Papers used by Boydell & Brewer are natural, recycled products made from
wood grown in sustainable forests.

Typeset in 9/11 pt Melior by Long House Publishing Services, Cumbria, UK
Printed in Great Britain
by CPI Group (UK) Ltd, Croydon CR0 4YY

Dedication

This issue of
African Literature Today
is dedicated to the memory of
Professor Emmanuel N. Obiechina

Our literary statesman, erudite and most
unassuming mentor; our revered 'Dean of African
Literary Criticism.' You taught us the medium, manner,
and mode. You will live eternally through
the protégés you nurtured consciously and
unconsciously on both sides of the Atlantic,
and by the indelible *footprints* you so richly
left for African Literature on the sands of time.
Farewell!

Contents

ix

Notes on Contributors

Helen Chukwuma, Professor of English at Jackson State University, Mississippi, has published widely in African Literature, Oral Literature, and Women's Studies including *Feminism in African Literature*, and a forthcoming book on *Women in Chinua Achebe's Fiction*.

Godini D. Darah is Professor of Oral Literature and Folklore in the Department of English and Literary Studies, Delta State University, Abraka, Nigeria. His publications include *Battles of Songs: Udje Tradition of the Urhobo* and *Radical Essays in Nigerian Literature*.

Blessing Diala-Ogamba is Associate Professor of English at Coppin State University, Baltimore, Maryland, USA. She has published articles on African Literature in refereed journals and anthologies in the United States and elsewhere. Her research interests are World Literature and Women's Literature.

Patricia T. Emenyonu, Assistant Editor of *African Literature Today*, teaches African Literature and Women's Studies in the Departments of English and Africana Studies, University of Michigan-Flint. She has published widely in refereed journals and anthologies, and is the author of *Reading and the Nigerian Cultural Background*.

Mark Ighile teaches in the Department of English, Redeemer's University, Ogun State, Nigeria, where he specializes in Oral Literature, Folklore Studies, and Performance Criticism. His research interests include Literary Stylistics and Criticism, Cultural Communication, and Bible as Literature.

Isaac V. Joslin is Visiting Assistant Professor of Francophone Literature and African Studies at St. Lawrence University, Canton, New York. His research and teaching interests center on African Literature and Cinema. He has published in *International Journal of Francophone Studies*, and *Contemporary French and Francophone Studies*.

Charles Nnolim is Professor of English at the University of Port Harcourt, Nigeria. A world acclaimed and renowned literary critic, Nnolim has published widely in the field of African Literature and Criticism. He is Associate Editor of *African Literature Today*.

Chimalum Nwankwo is Professor of Literature in the Department of English, North Carolina A & T University, Greensboro. A scholar-poet (uniquely known as 'poet of the aerial zone'), versatile and seasoned academic, Chimalum Nwankwo has published widely on African Literature and Criticism in leading journals in the field in Africa, United Kingdom and United States. He has produced five collections of poetry including notably *The Womb in the Heart and Other Poems*, and *Of the Deepest Shadows and the Prisons of Time* (2010).

Eustace Palmer is Professor of English and Coordinator of Africana Studies at Georgia College and State University. One of the pre-eminent pioneer critics of African Literature, Palmer has published over sixty articles and four books on African Literature including a seminal work, *An Introduction to the African Novel* (1972). He is also author of three novels – *A Hanging is Announced, Canfira's Travels*, and *A Tale of Three Women*. Eustace Palmer was named Georgia College and State University Distinguished Professor for 2010/2011.

Anna Serafin, an independent scholar, had taught Literature at secondary level for decades in several states in the United States. She has presented papers on African Literature and Film at several international conferences and workshops in the United Kingdom and the United States. Her publications have appeared in *The English Journal*, *The Multicultural Review*, and *African Renaissance*.

Peter Wuteh Vakunta teaches French Literature and Francophone Literature and Cultures at the Defense Language Institute, Presiddio of Monterey, California. He has published articles in *Research in African Literatures*, *Journal of African Literature Association* (*JALA*), *Journal of Midwest Modern Language Association*, and *Translation Review*.

Ernest N. Emenyonu

The theme of this issue of *African Literature Today*, 'Teaching African Literature', was conceived as a tribute to renowned veteran teachers/ scholars world-wide who blazed the trail and overcame every obstacle to carve out a pride of place for African literature in the Academy in the second half of the twentieth century. Sixteen of these eminent scholars were identified from the United Kingdom, the United States, Africa, Japan, India, Australia, Germany, Canada, and Sweden. Each was invited on 30 October 2009, to take time to write and submit an article on the experience of teaching African literature at whatever level or geographic location over the years.

The idea was that by reporting their various experiences (what worked and what didn't) in teaching African Literature dating back to the middle of the twentieth century, they would be passing on concrete skills and legacies to younger colleagues in the profession. Their reports would also be indisputable affirmations and validations of the global presence of African literature in the Academy. This would also be an invaluable service to the discipline of African literature. In the same vein, the theme of this issue was envisioned as a logical sequel to the world-wide celebration of Chinua Achebe's *Things Fall Apart* in 2008. For indeed, *Things Fall Apart* was the catalyst that led to the opening of doors for African Literature in the curriculum of educational systems all over the world. That novel made the literary world take serious notice for the first time, of the emerging voices of imaginative creativity from the continent of Africa. These new voices were 'loaded' with innovative thematic and refreshingly stylistic versatilities that energized and added colour to contemporary World Literature, particularly Anglophone and Francophone literatures.

It was gratifying that of the 16 veteran scholars/teachers of African literature contacted in October 2009, as many as 13 enthusiastically accepted to contribute articles to this volume. However, when the articles were due a year later in October 2010, only one fulfilled his promise. We salute Professor Eustace Palmer for his continued pioneering role and inimitable dedication to the cause of African literature. His pioneering role has been nothing short of historic, heroic and legendary. His 175-page *Introduction to the African Novel* (1972, Heinemann), was one of the most authoritative early works on the criticism of African Literature. It became an invaluable handbook not only for beginning scholars and critics of African Literature, but also (especially) for teachers inside and outside Africa who greatly needed guidance in the pedagogical approaches to the emerging African creative works. Its publication was timely and helped to shape the nature, tone, direction and dynamics of African literary criticism at a crucial point in time.

The contributors to this volume have stepped in to fill the gaps. They have performed a most laudable rescue mission surpassing all expectations. They have in each of their contributions provided profound insights into the challenges of teaching African literature in various geographic locations, the nature of the learners of African literature, and the impact of African creative works on them as individuals. They have discussed the use of modern technology in the teaching of African literature and the resilient impacts of African Oral Literature on both teachers and learners. The teaching of African literature, like any other major world literature, remains as challenging as it is exciting and rewarding.

In the twenty-first century, there is enough evidence to state that the teaching of African literature in all parts of the world is something that should be advocated for the best interest of posterity in general and the field of contemporary World literature in particular. The case for the literary excellence of African fiction has been sufficiently and incontrovertibly made. In the last two decades of the twentieth century, African creative writers ostensibly immortalized African literature irrevocably in the annals of World literary history with achievements too hard to ignore anymore. In 1986 Wole Soyinka (Nigeria) became the first African to win the Nobel Prize for Literature. He was followed by Naguib Mahfouz (Egypt) in 1988, and three years later, Nadine Gordimer (South Africa) in 1991. This apparently unstoppable winning streak continued into the new millennium with J.M. Coetzee (South Africa) winning the Prize in 2003. And one can state without fear of contradiction that Doris Lessing who won the prize in 2007 has self-acknowledged real and symbolic African roots and influences in her imaginative creativity. That is why in this issue of the journal we have reason to celebrate the teaching of African literature both inside and outside the continent of Africa.

The title of this Editorial Article is adapted from the title of a historic literary celebration at Syracuse University, New York, October 14-16, 2010. A valedictory symposium entitled '50 Years of African Literature in the Academy' was organized by the University in honour of the retiring renowned William Safire Professor of Modern Letters, Prof. M.J.C. Echeruo, one of the most formidable 'founding fathers' in the field of the criticism and teaching of African literature. If this journal had a 'Congressional Medal of Honor' for the year 2010, it would incontestably go to Syracuse University. Instead of the all-too-familiar convention of honouring a retiring famous professor with a valedictory speech/lecture given by him followed by a dinner or cocktail, Syracuse University chose (most wisely) to assemble a team of scholars to reflect, theorize and philosophize on the half a century of African Literature in the Academy. It was a grand success. What did not come out as forcefully and emphatically as it should have, was the place or role of Professor Echeruo in the '50 Years of African literature in the Academy'.

M.J.C. Echeruo has made towering contributions in the establishment of an indelible identity for African literature as a significant literary canon in the Academy, and the herculean trail blazing task of charting a road map for its successful inclusion in the literature curriculum of tertiary institutions inside and outside Africa. The incredible amount of resources he has put at the disposal of young scholars in African literature as well as his relentless mentoring of budding African creative artists remain impossible to be sufficiently described or documented in so short a space. Whenever a ground-breaking literary phenomenon was contemplated in the years that he was in the Nigerian university system, Professor Echeruo was invited to shape and structure it and design its future direction. This was the case when he was invited in 1979 to give the maiden edition of the pan-Igbo annual lecture series known today as 'The Ahiajoku Lecture' held in November every year. His lecture, 'A Matter of Identity' served to define the purpose, objectives, and goals of the annual lecture conceived broadly to identify and define the Igbo contributions to world civilization. Similarly, when the Imo State government of Nigeria (his home state) decided to found a university, they tapped Professor Echeruo as its foundation vice-chancellor. In these and other similar intellectual endeavors, he always found a way to carve a major place for African literary studies!

The Syracuse Symposium attracted a galaxy of high profile authorities on African Literature – Abiola Irele, Biodun Jeifo, Micere Githae Mugo, Obiora Udechukwu, Kenneth Harrow, Tejumola Olaniyan, Lokangaka Lasambe, Anthonia Kalu, Maik Nwosu, Obi Nwakanma, and a host of others from within and outside the United States. And to bridge the gap between the 'yesterdays' and 'todays' in African creative writing, the major keynote speaker was the indomitable, sparkling and vibrant new voice – the author of *Half of a Yellow Sun* – Chimamanda Ngozi Adichie. However, the cynosure of all eyes at the forum was the elder statesman, the inimitable literary scholar, critic and teacher, Prof. Emmanuel Obiechina.

I stayed very close to Professor Obiechina for the two days of the symposium. He had been for me, like for many others of my generation, a willing mentor at all times, the imperceptible voice and hand that guided and motivated every inch of the way. He chaired plenary sessions at the symposium, led discussions when he was not chairing and was surrounded even during tea breaks by bubbling young scholars seeking to get a close view of him, hear him tell them directly the rich literary theories they had been reading from his books. Professor Obiechina had time for everybody at the symposium. All of us were woken up two weeks later with the shocking news of his death! He had e-mailed most of us at the end of the symposium to indicate that he had a new e-mail address. He requested each one of us to respond to that e-mail address so that he would be sure it reached us. Most did. I was reliably informed that the last thing he did on that fateful night in November 2010, was to read through his e-mails.

In a short memorial tribute I recalled his ubiquitous mesmeric presence at the Syracuse Symposium in these words:

> Only 'yesterday,' it seems, we were together at Syracuse and shared the bounty of your wit and wisdom surrounded by eminent scholars of the Academy. And when the Symposium was over, you told me about your recent trip to Nigeria (returning the day before the Symposium) for the historic induction into the first-ever Nigerian Academy of Letters' *Hall of Fame*. It was an honor no one deserved better although you tried to play it down. You taught us the literary medium, the manner and mode of its criticism; you groomed us in the craft and tenderly pampered us even as we groped about the way trying to emulate your wit and wisdom ... You will live eternally through the protégés you have nurtured on both sides of the Atlantic ...

In 1994 I was asked by the Imo State Government in Nigeria to introduce Professor Obiechina as the Ahiajoku Lecturer of the year. Part of my introduction had this to say:

> His fertile erudition has given birth to countless scholarly works on African Literature, scores of original articles in learned journals all over the world, public lectures in arenas stretching from Nigeria to Europe, North America, Asia, Latin American and the West Indies ... If a topic is important in Commonwealth Literature; if a topic is crucial in African Literature, it cannot be completely so until Emmanuel Obiechina has spoken or written about it, and when he does, it immediately confers respectability and authenticity to that particular point of view ... Professor Emmanuel Obiechina is to all who know him – all who have read him, and all who have experienced the vibrancy of his mind and intellect, truly the teachers' Teacher, the scholars' Scholar, the professors' Professor, the critics' Critic, the writers' Writer and the authors' Author ... It is impossible to adequately introduce Professor Emmanuel Obiechina. It is impossible for me to describe in words, the dignity of this man, his intellect and the depth of his vision as a literary scholar, a philosopher and a humanist ...

It is for these reasons and many more that this issue of *African Literature Today* on 'Teaching African Literature' is deservedly dedicated to the memory of Professor Emmanuel Obiechina.

'There goes Emmanuel Obiechina ...
there never was, and never will be *another* like him.'
Farewell!!

Teaching Ben Okri's *The Famished Road* & Syl Cheney-Coker's *The Last Harmattan of Alusine Dunbar*

Eustace Palmer

Ben Okri's prize-winning novel *The Famished Road* and Syl Cheney-Coker's *The Last Harmattan of Alusine Dunbar* are, without doubt, among the most challenging works of African literature to teach. The reasons for this are not far to seek. First, there is the enormous bulk of both novels. In an age when teachers complain about the attention span of students and most novels run for no more than about three hundred pages, the teaching of works, which, in the case of *The Last Harmattan* runs for almost four hundred pages of extremely concentrated and even poetic prose and, in the case of *The Famished Road*, goes on for almost five hundred pages of repetitive events, must surely pose special problems. The second reason is a rather simple and mundane one: that of availability. This is particularly relevant to Cheney-Coker's novel, since *The Famished Road* is generally available in Anchor Books paperback. Both works have, of course, become classics of African literature, but classics of African literature, which need to feature in courses on African literature, do not necessarily have the kind of perennial and universal appeal that would make publishers (largely Western ones), who always have an eye on their bottom line, wish to continue publishing them after the first printing runs out. Cheney-Coker's *The Last Harmattan* seems to have suffered that fate. The third reason is the preponderance in both novels of elements of magical realism and the use of the supernatural and the fantastic which seems to strain the credibility of many readers. It is the purpose of this paper to throw out a few tentative hints that might facilitate the teaching of both works and make the exercise ultimately rewarding. These hints result from teaching these novels in courses here in the United Sates over a number of years.

The first suggestion I would like to make is that both these novels ought to be taught at the graduate level and several sessions should be devoted to each. The sheer bulk of both works might create some daunting challenges at the undergraduate level, and they both raise theoretical issues that can only be fully appreciated and thoroughly discussed at the graduate level. Concepts of realism and postmodernity can, of course, be handled at the undergraduate level, but they are surely discussed much more rewardingly at the graduate level, and both novels raise these issues in large measure.

It is very tempting to see both these novels as 'postmodern' works, therefore the starting point of the discussion should revolve around the extent to which Okri and Cheney-Coker were postmodern in intention; one of my graduate students, fresh from exposure to contemporary critical theories, exclaimed that *The Famished Road* was undoubtedly 'postmodern.' Of course, one cannot discuss postmodernism in isolation from modernism, since postmodernism was a reaction to modernism, in the sense that it continued, sometimes to an extreme as Abrams and Harpham have said, the countertraditional experiments of modernism, but also sought ways to break away from some modernist forms, particularly the 'elitism' of modernist 'high art' and thereby have recourse to 'mass culture' forms in films, television, newspaper cartoons and popular music. According to Abrams and Geoffrey Harpham, 'many of the works of postmodern literature ... so blend literary genres, cultural and stylistic levels, the serious and the playful, that they resist classification according to traditional literary rubrics' (203).

With this definition in mind, to what extent can one say that *The Famished Road* and *The Last Harmattan* are postmodern? The basis for the suggestion is that they both rely very heavily on the use of the supernatural and the magical and *The Famished Road*, in particular, is narrated by an 'abiku' child, a child supposedly from the spirit world. Both novelists, according to some critics, do so because they wish to break away from the modernist Eurocentric narrative of history. It would mean that writers like Okri and Cheney-Coker were consciously reacting against modernism and all that it implies. However, we must be aware that modernism and all the literary and artistic baggage that it involved may not have the same resonance for African writers that it does for Western writers; African writers are dealing with a completely different set of issues and not with the cataclysmic breakdown of society and values that modernism involved. They would not therefore necessarily have to explore postmodernist techniques as a reaction to modernism. It is therefore rather simplistic to label their works as 'postmodern.' John Hawley, for instance, says, 'the significance of an abiku narrator ... is that it moves African literature closer to the postmodern movement' (31). He does realize that there may be problems in regarding some African writers as postmodernists, but he insists that such a label would be helpful because these writers do two things that are typical of postmodernist writing: 'they resist the European master narrative of history' and 'they are markedly experimental in their narration, carrying into their fiction many of the postmodern literary characteristics' (35-36). Maggi Phillips suggests that *The Famished Road* is the expression of a genuine 'third world consciousness' and thus implies that Okri's main concern was aesthetic (44-45). Olatubosun Ogunsanwo states that Okri is concerned with 'the literary aesthetic of truth telling ... the whole issue of the aesthetic and epistemological premises of literary realism' (40). In other words, Okri was merely looking for a literary format that would more truthfully convey African realism as he saw it, more truthfully, that is, than the worn-out Eurocentric narrative. John Hawley goes even further to claim that Okri 'has an aesthetic, rather than an overtly political or psychological aim' (32).

These critics, then, see Okri's main preoccupations as being aesthetic rather than social, political or psychological: the leading concerns of most novelists. They see *The Famished Road* as signalling Okri's attempt to bring the African novel in line with postmodernity. However, we must, as always, be cautious in applying the latest Western critical terminology to African writing, as Okri himself has suggested. The fact that postmodernism is very much in vogue does not mean that we must apply it to every literary work that seems exploratory or innovatory, no matter where it comes from. In The *Famished Road* Okri is certainly experimental and could be said to have moved away from the 'European master narrative of history,' but that does not mean that he is being consciously postmodern. He has used techniques that are very similar to those used by Amos Tutuola fifty years ago in *The Palm-wine Drinkard.* Are we to say that Tutuola, too, was being 'postmodern'?

It is the argument of this paper that Okri, in fact, is being not only aesthetic, but also social, political and psychological, and that the entire work, from start to finish, is concerned with social comment, with the state of contemporary Nigeria, and that it is to this end that he uses the abiku child as narrator and presents the mystical experiences of that child. I would also suggest, in fact, that effective teaching of this novel should start with a reading of Tutuola's *The Palm-wine Drinkard,* if members of the class have not already read it, for them to see how another African writer, who had nothing to do with postmodernism, uses beings from the spirit world and shows a human being interacting with them. The course should also take a look at the different representations of the 'Abiku' concept in poems by Wole Soyinka and John Pepper Clark. In Soyinka's poem the abiku child is a defiant exultant child rejoicing in the misery it causes its parents and daring them to do their worst to try to retain it in this world, while in the Clark poem the narrator pleads with the child to stay because its mother's womb is exhausted. The situation in *The Famished Road* is closer to that in the Clark poem.

This brings us to the main rationale for the use of the abiku child as narrator: it is simply that the novel is, in a sense, allegorical, the child being a representative of the young state of Nigeria which, socially and politically, keeps on oscillating between prosperity and stability on the one hand, and misery and anarchy on the other, but which must make up its mind to stay, just as the abiku child keeps coming to this world and going back to the spirit world, but must decide, on the pleas of its parents, to stay at last in the human world. This is one of the first and most important points that any teaching of the novel must make to the students. In this respect, it is the other abiku child in the novel, Ade, who holds the key to the significance of the abiku and to Okri's decision to use the abiku as protagonist and narrator. Towards the end of the novel he makes some very significant comments:

> 'Trouble is always coming. Maybe it's just as well, 'he said. 'Your story has just begun. Mine is ending. I want to go to my other home. Your mother Is right; there is too much unnecessary suffering on this earth....My time is coming. I have worn out my mother's womb and now she can't have any more children. Coming and going, I have seen the world, I have seen the future. The Koran says nothing is ever finished."
> 'What will happen?' I asked him.
> Quivering, biting his lips till he drew blood, he said:
> 'There will be the rebirth of a father. A man with seven heads will take you away. You will come back. You will stay. Before that the spirits and our ancestors will hold a great meeting to discuss the future of the world. It will be one of the most important meetings ever held. Suffering is coming. There will be wars and famine. Terrible things will happen. New diseases, hunger, the rich eating up the people, people poisoning the sky and the waters, people going mad in the name of history, the clouds will breathe fire, the spirit of things will dry up, laughter will become strange.'...
> 'There will be changes. Coups, soldiers everywhere. Ugliness. Blindness. And then when people least expect it a great transformation will take place in the world. Suffering people will know justice and beauty. A wonderful change is coming from far away and people will realize the great meaning of struggle and hope. There will be peace. Then people will forget. Then it will all start again, getting worse, getting better. Don't fear. You will always have something to struggle for, even if it is beauty or joy.'...
> 'Our country is an abiku country. Like the spirit child, it keeps coming and going. One day it will decide to remain. It will become strong. I won't see it.'
> (477-8)

How can anyone read this and say that Okri's main concern is merely aesthetic? Evidently the novel is firmly located in the arena of social comment and Okri is preoccupied with the social, political and economic problems confronting not only Nigeria, but the world as a whole. This gives the novel a formidable universality and explains the worldwide acclamation it has received.

The next major issue that any teaching of both *The Famished Road* and *The Last Harmattan* should get to grips with is the concept of magical realism. Both novels are a unique blend of the apparently supernatural or magical or mystical with the obviously realistic. They therefore raise questions about the nature of reality or realism, which has been taken to be one of the hallmarks of the novel form, and most critics confront the issue by discussing these novels within the context of magical realism. For instance, Edna Aizenberg gives a definition of magical realism that enables her to include *The Famished Road* within its boundaries. She sees the magical realist text as being, like Okri's abiku child, 'caught in the interspace between the spirit world and the living – roughly the magic and the real' (28). Renato Oliva sees magical realist literature as blurring the boundaries beween the land of the living and the world of the dead, as Okri's abiku does (174). Magical realism is, of course, most closely associated with the Hispanic world and Latin America, since many critics see it as having originated in Spain. In works from these cultures, elements that would normally be considered supernatural or even fantastic mingle freely with the normally realistic and both are accepted as real by the people within the environment presented in the works. The reader also is forced to accept them as such because the strange, supernatural, otherworldly, and fantastic are made to appear familiar and part of the normal order of things. As I have suggested in my book, *Of War and Women, Oppression and Optimism*, the most important aspect of magical realism is that it forces us to examine our notions of what is real (226). And this is the point that the class should discuss: the notion that reality might be culture based or even multi-faceted. The modern Western world, taking its cue from science, has insisted that reality must be objective, tangible, scientifically provable, or demonstrable. Other notions of reality, however, ask us to include within its boundaries phenomena that might be otherwise considered supernatural, fantastic, mystical, or magical. It also asks us to question our mode of apprehension of what is real. Who is to say that ghosts do not exist or that there aren't some people who possess supernatural powers? Even in Western society, there have been times when people believed in spirits, and witches.

Magical realism asks us to see that concepts of the real have always differed according to time and place and that, although modern Western technological society has placed rigid boundaries between the 'real' and the 'super-real,' the distinction for some other societies is not that clear cut. In various African societies beings from the spirit world are supposed to hover around and mingle freely with human beings, and there are certain human beings who have the ability to see such spirits and communicate with them. A writer therefore who presents such beings is not being unrealistic or fantastic. He is merely presenting another order of reality.

Of course, it can be argued that, if for some societies, such phenomena are regarded as real, then the term 'magical' should not be applied to them at all. This is, in fact, the position of Syl Cheney-Coker who also makes extensive use of these elements in the first part of *The Last Harmattan*. In a recent conversation with the present writer at the annual conference of the African Literature Association held in Morgantown, West Virginia, Cheney-Coker robustly objected to the use of the term 'magical.' For him, these phenomena represent another order of reality, and he told the story, once told him by his mother, of a woman who had definitely died in one location and who was discovered to be living in another location, only to disappear when someone from her previous home turned up and recognized her. For these people, the incident was real, not magical. The job of the author narrating such an incident is to convince the reader of its reality. We will turn to this later.

It would also be necessary to discuss whether the term 'magical realism' should be applied to African writers like Okri and Cheney-Coker at all since, in the minds of some critics, it is a peculiarly Hispanic phenomenon supposed to have originated in the Iberian Peninsula and associated with Hispanic and Latin American writers like Gabriel Garcia Marquez, whose story 'A very Old Man with Enormous Wings' is well known. In that story, a ragged old angel has a mishap as he is coming to earth for the soul of a young child and breaks his wings in consequence. The angel's scruffy wings and antique appearance are very powerfully and realistically described. Since he looks very much like a chicken, he is kept in a chicken coop by the parents of the young child, who mysteriously revives, probably because the old angel is unable to complete his mission and get her soul. The people in the environment accept the old man as real, and, after living with the child's parents for a considerable period, he eventually regains the power of his wings and flies away. The main ingredients of magical realism are certainly present here: the juxtaposition of the realistic (in the description of the ragged old man) with the extraordinary (in that he has wings that enable him to fly to earth to come for the child's soul and eventually to fly away).   The people also accept him as real and the events are described in such a way that the reader is compelled to suspend disbelief.

However, it is possible to contest the view that magical realism originated in the Iberian Peninsula and should be exclusively associated with Hispanic or Latin American literature. Stories of ghosts, spirits, and human beings with extraordinary or even supernatural powers have existed in Africa since the dawn of time, and, before Marquez, Fagunwa and Amos Tutuola in works such as *The Forest of a Thousand Demons* and *The Palm-Wine Drinkard* represented these in literature. In any case, where the concept originated is irrelevant; the important point is that it is to be found in both literatures and maybe even in other literatures, and neither Cheney-Coker nor Okri could be said to be derivative. Although Cheney-Coker has acknowledged his debt to Marquez and other Latin American writers in other respects, there is no doubt that, as far as the concept of magical realism is concerned, he was influenced by sources in his own tradition. The important issue is why both authors use magical realist elements.

In *The Famished Road*, then, Okri presents us with a protagonist in Azaro who is an abiku child and who represents the young struggling country of Nigeria. Just as the abiku child is being constantly pulled and tempted by his spirit companions to go back to the spirit world and leave the hostile, corrupt and anarchic world to which he has come and with which he has cast his lot, so the young state of Nigeria will be engaged in an unending tug of war between the forces of progress and retrogression, stability and anarchy, but the hope is held out that eventually it will, like the abiku child, stay and remain strong. This is the main reason for Okri's use of the abiku child as the narrator protagonist; and since the abiku child will be engaged in a constant tussle with his spirit companions in the world of the unborn to get him to leave the realistic and unsympathetic human world, there will be plenty of opportunities for the use of magical realism, which will, in fact, occupy most of the first part of the novel.

The Abiku child Ade's prophetic and mystical comments towards the end suggest that the problems that the Abiku Azaro will view are not just confined to Nigeria, but are, in fact, universal. In this connection, effective teaching of this novel must confront the concept of the road and the title 'The Famished Road.' Discussion of the significance of the road in Yoruba mythology will be absolutely relevant here, and reference must certainly be made to Soyinka's famous poem 'Death in the Dawn' in the collection *Idanre and Other Poems*, from which the title almost certainly comes. The relevant verse reads thus:

The right foot for joy, the left, dread
And the mother prayed, Child
May you never walk
When the road waits, famished. (11)

It will also be useful to ask students to read Soyinka's play, 'The Road.' From these, it will be seen that the road is regarded as a voracious predatory supernatural force waiting to pounce on its unsuspecting victims. Okri takes over this conception of the road as a predatory and exploitative force that demands propitiatory sacrifice. For instance, Azaro's father tells him the story, almost certainly taken from the oral tradition, of the monstrous and insatiable King of the road who even ended up devouring himself. Yet, 'he is still hungry, and he will always be hungry. That is why there are so many accidents in the world' (261). But the road also obviously means the greedy world, and the King of the road is linked with the predatory Landlord in the novel and the politicians who exploit the people.

However, Okri's treatment of the subject goes far beyond this. The novel's opening statement reads thus: 'In the beginning there was a river. The river became a road and the road branched out to the whole world. And because the road was once a river it was always hungry' (3). The road is therefore linked with the river, which is also presented as a potentially destructive force gloating in its own power: 'A river, roaring and delighted with the prospect of fresh destruction, descended on the land, smashed the houses, felled the trees, which instantly grew and destroyed sections of the enchanting road' (331). Something strange seems to have happened here; the potentially destructive road has now become the 'enchanting road.' This suggests that the road is not always a negative force; indeed, it could itself be destroyed by the river.

Other sections of the novel suggest that the river represents destiny, which rivers have always suggested in several cultures. Thus the King, in pronouncing the child's destiny says, 'You will cause no end of trouble. You will travel many roads before you find the river of your destiny' (6). Madame Koto in blessing the boy says, 'The road will never swallow you. The river of your destiny will always overcome evil' (46). Toward the end of the novel there is reference to a duiker being sacrificed for 'the opening of the road of Madame Koto's destiny' (458). In being associated with the river, then, the road, like the river, also represents destiny. In being identified with destiny, the road and the river represent what happens to one in this life, the options that one has and the choices that one makes. But because it represents choices made, the road, in particular, can represent a lifestyle, a way of life, a culture, or a civilization. This is why, when the perceptive and precocious Azaro looks into the eyes of the duiker that is to be sacrificed to the opening of Madame Koto's destiny's road, he has a vision during which he sees this:

> Deep in the duiker's eyes, I ran through the yellow forests, through deluded generations, through time. I witnessed the destruction of great shrines, the death of mighty trees that housed centuries of insurgent as well as soothing memories, sacred texts, alchemical secrets of wizards, and potent herbs. I saw the forests die. I saw the people grow smaller in being. I saw the death of their many roads and ways and philosophies. (457)

In fact, the road represents ways of life, cultures, and civilizations. With respect to the individual it represents life itself and the experiences of life: life that can be destructive and miserable and might swallow the individual, or life that can also be pleasant and fulfilling.

Since the first sentence of the novel states that the road branched out to the whole world, there is the suggestion that the road embraces the whole world and therefore the whole of human life itself. Indeed, it can also be said to represent time and history. Since the road is associated with the river, and rivers are, by their very nature almost prehistoric and suggest the march of time, the road itself, by association, represents the march of time and history. This is confirmed by a very significant episode in the novel. After a rather merciless beating by Dad, the boy becomes ill and decides to take revenge on his parents by attempting to withdraw from life and listen to the seductive appeal of his spirit companions. He goes into a trance in which he and a three-headed spirit travel together and come to a 'Mighty green road' (326). During a lengthy conversation with the three-headed spirit the latter tells the boy that the road is being built by a people whose prophet told them that the road cannot be finished because the moment it is finished all of them will perish. When the boy asks why, the spirit goes on:

'I suppose they will have nothing to do, nothing to dream for, and no need for a future. They will perish of completeness, of boredom. The road is their soul, the soul of their history. That is why, when they have built a long section of it, or forgotten the words of their prophet and begun to think they have completed it, landquakes happen, lightning strikes, invisible volcanoes erupt, rivers descend on them, hurricanes tear up their earth, the road goes mad and twists and destroys itself, or the people become distorted in spirit and start to turn the road into other things, or the workers go insane, the people start wars, revolts cripple everything and a thousand things distract them and wreck what they have built and a new generation comes along and begins again from the wreckage.' (329-30)

This road, then, sums up the whole of human experience. It is a road that epitomizes the paradoxes of human existence: it is both endless and has an end; it leads to the world of human beings and the world of spirits, to both heaven and hell. It has taken two thousand years to build, but its construction will, apparently, never be completed, because human civilization and human history will always go on.

Two thousand years is the age of Christianity, and this particular road has connections with heaven and there is talk of a prophet who asks a particular people to build this road to heaven. Obviously, this road that is being built towards heaven represents perfection or the perfect but unattainable life. The road can therefore never be finished. Human society, human life, and human history can never be perfect. Whenever people, in their delusion or pride, assume that they have finished building the road or think they have achieved perfection, all kinds of disasters, natural as well as man-made, happen to remind them that there could never be perfection and the cycle of human history or progress begins all over again. Each generation begins with nothing and with everything. They know all the earlier mistakes, all the earlier intentions, all the early dreams. 'They have an affinity of hope and an eternity of struggles' (330). The whole is an allegory of human life, human history, and human progress. This is what the road really represents.

On a very mundane level, the road obviously represents the back alley where the boy and his parents and a number of other under-privileged individuals live, constantly bothered by the predatory landlord and exploited by unscrupulous politicians. This is hardly surprising, since the famished road of the title suggests that the novel in general is about the potentially destructive impact of life, time and history on human beings. Life, for most individuals in general, and for Nigerians in particular, seems to be miserable and fraught with oppression, deprivation, and exploitation. The novel, as we have seen, very much constitutes social comment. Human misery is partly the consequence of the fact that human society can never be perfect. But this does not mean that we must not keep on striving for perfection. The very fact that the road can never be finished means that there are all kinds of possibilities. Every individual can do his or her utmost to put an end to exploitation, tyranny, oppression, and suffering in general and strive to attain the best that they could possibly be. There is always 'the probability that no injustice lasts for ever, no love ever dies, that no light is ever really extinguished, that no road is ever complete, that no way is ever definitive, no truth ever final, and that there are never really any beginnings or endings' (488). Human history will continue to proceed in cycles not in a straight path, as periods of anarchy and chaos are succeeded by others of peace, justice and love. Neither will last forever; the road will never be complete.

In teaching *The Famished Road,* one will have to confront the relationship between the much longer first section of the novel and the shorter second section. The first section is much longer because it is largely about the attempts of the abiku child to resist attempts to seduce him back to the spirit world, although he himself has made a very conscious decision to stay in the human world, fraught though that world is with suffering, misery, exploitation, unhappiness and tyranny. Since the beings that are trying to seduce or compel Azaro to return are spirits, this section is shot through with magical encounters that some might well find repetitive. However, they are all necessary, because the beings that are trying to get the boy back are extremely powerful and tenacious; they are determined not to give up their attempts, just as the boy is determined to stay in the human world. Readers must also have at the backs of their minds that, on an allegorical level, the boy's struggles represent the young Nigerian state's struggle to survive in the modern world. That is by no means an easy task. Even in the first section, we see the corruption, exploitation, deprivation and social inequalities that characterize the young Nigerian state and that are obstacles to stability. These must be, and are, forcefully presented. The view of some readers that the first part is entirely taken up with the marvelous while the second deals with the realistic political and social issues that contemporary Nigeria has to face is surely erroneous. There is a tremendous amount of social comment in the first part, just as the second has its fair share of the marvellous. After all, it is in the first part that we encounter the rats, who symbolize society's predators, the malevolent creditors, and the exploitative landlord, not to mention the unscrupulous politicians who give the people bad milk; and in the second part, we have the activities of spirits like the three headed spirit. The fact is that the boy makes his decision to stay, not just in spite of the tenacious attempts of his spirit companions to entice him back, but also in spite of the misery, suffering, poverty, and social inequalities that he sees in the human world. His parents' own experiences are a testament to that.

Having cast his lot with the human world and decided to stay, the boy then proceeds in the second section to give valuable support to his father, who now becomes the champion of the people's cause and fights to put an end to the poverty, exploitation and suffering we had witnessed in plenty in the first part. In teaching this novel one should also be able to demonstrate the abiku narrator's gradual development and change. In order to represent this development convincingly, Okri has to depict numerous magical and other episodes.

The teaching of *The Famished Road* should also involve discussion of the methods Okri uses to impart credibility in spite of the preponderance of magical elements. The most important of these is, of course, the use of the spirit child himself as the narrator/protagonist. Had the events been narrated in the third person by an omniscient narrator, it might have been difficult to induce the reader to suspend disbelief. But from the very beginning they are narrated by the spirit child himself who tells us of his history and background, and we feel we are getting it all from the horse's mouth, as it were. It is therefore difficult to 'disbelieve.' The use of a spirit child with strange powers from another world means that he can view the chaos of the normal human world with fresh eyes and insight, especially since, in the African context, this kind of child is believed to be capable of seeing all these facets of reality. As Okri himself says, 'if you accept the premise that this kid is an abiku, a spirit child, it's not unnatural that he would see spirits' (Ross 337). The use of the abiku as narrator thus makes for the enhancement of realism.

In teaching this novel, one should be prepared to demonstrate the narrator/protagonist's gradual development, particularly as he struggles to resist the attempts of his spirit companions to entice him to return. After all, this is what the first section is mostly concerned with. Perhaps one should begin this section with a statement that according to Yoruba cosmology, the universe consists of three worlds: the world of the unborn, the world of the living, and the world of the departed. Many of the spirits Azaro has to contend with come from the world of the unborn. He himself originally came from that world, and his companions are trying to entice him to return to it. It does not take the reader long to discover that Azaro is a most remarkable, even precocious, child, with extraordinary powers of perception. He can see things that normal human beings can't. He can see right through people to discern the insincerity, duplicity and fraud underneath and, what is even more important, he is bold enough to tell them about their real moral qualities to their faces. He is bold enough to tell the landlord to his face that he is a thief, not a chief, and he has no qualms about deliberately throwing stones at the window of one of the annoying creditors. He is capable of daring his spirit companions to do their worst and to tell his father's insulting opponent in a game of draughts to shut up. He can certainly speak up for himself and is capable of fighting off the attempts of those who are trying to kidnap him, whether they are spirits or human beings. This boy is certainly not passive.

In the light of this, it is astonishing that Derek Wright, in his article on the novel, should declare that 'Azaro is a peculiarly passive and power-less character who performs very few actions, most of them inconse-quential' (23). This must surely be one of the most egregious claims made in the whole history of the criticism of African literature. One wonders whether Derek Wright could be reading the same novel. How can one claim that a boy, who actually fights off the attempts of spirits to kidnap him, challenges creditors and even the landlord, and makes a deliberate decision to stay on in the human world against all odds and against the tenacious attempts of his spirit companions to woo him back, is passive and powerless and does nothing of consequence? It is, in fact, vital to Okri's conception to see that Azaro does a lot of things that are consequential. Margaret Cezair-Thompson seems to have a much better grasp of the novel and hits the mark much more accurately when she mentions Azaro's resourcefulness, particularly in 'constructing an inviolable identity' (42).

Let us first of all recognize that Azaro is an extremely young boy. When the novel starts he could hardly be more than about six or seven; all the more reason why his resourcefulness is so astonishing. This can be seen, for instance, in the scene where he has his first experience with the spirits in Madame Koto's bar. He goes boldly to Madame Koto and tells her that her bar is full of spirits, and the language used suggests the boldness and audacity of the exercise. Madame Koto apparently wishes to do nothing about it; in fact, it seems likely that in an attempt to carry on a prosperous trade, she has deliberately attracted the spirits to the bar by hanging up a particular fetish. The boy is intelligent and perceptive enough to realize that it is the fetish that is attracting the spirits, and he cleverly finds a way to seize it. He also recognizes these spirits as the creatures who abducted him the last time, and he wishes to protect himself by pre-empting their strike. Not only does he seize the fetish to nullify its effect and that of the spirits, he buries it and marks the spot. This gives him the upper hand over the powerful Madame Koto and the spirits, whose bodies now seem to dissolve in the rain. The measure of his growth is suggested by the fact that when he goes out next time he does not get lost, and he is able to survey the damage done by the rain on the people of the compound and find his way home against tremendous odds. The last time he got lost, his father beat him severely on his return; now, as though to acknowledge his growth, his father welcomes him pleasantly, his mother prepares a succulent dish, and they all three sit down and eat from the same bowl in peace and amity.

Later, Azaro wanders along the road deliberately; he gets lost, but this time he is able to find his way home again, and he now begins to enjoy getting lost because of the thrill of finding his way home again. A very significant stage now takes place in Azaro's development as he has an experience that could only be described as an epiphany. On one of his wanderings into unknown territory, he blunders into the marketplace and observes labourers carrying bags of garri and cement and looking like slaves. He gets a tremendous insight into the world's inequities as he realizes that these labourers and carriers are being forced to degrade themselves because of extreme poverty. But, above all, he has a revelation;

he sees a labourer who is being insulted by an unfeeling and merciless world and recognizes the suffering labourer as none other than his father, tottering under an excruciatingly heavy load of cement and insulted by the rest of the world. Though stunned by the terror of this discovery, he has the courage to shout out, 'Dad! No!' The father turns round, recognizes his son, and is overwhelmed with shame: 'tears streamed from his eyes, and there was shame on his face as he staggered right past me, almost crushing me with his might buckling feet' (148-9).

Dad eventually falls, and his falling is significant. He falls, not just under the weight of the cement which represents the world's unfairness, but under the weight of humiliation. The man who will later become a dreaded boxer and the champion of the people's cause is brought down to the lowest level he will ever know, and his nakedness is, as it were, revealed for his only son to see. For this son, it is an epiphany, a moment of illumination: 'For the first time in my life I had seen one of the sources of my father's misery' (149).

Azaro's development continues as he makes advances in his spiritual life. He learns to levitate himself out of his body and go through the roof, and as he flies he learns to control his motions. This very active boy now devises strategies not only for outwitting the thugs in his compound, but also the spirits in Madame Koto's bar and other places. Two episodes now follow that, with their initiatory and ritualistic aura, confirm the boy's gradual growth and development. In the first, he gets involved in a particularly lascivious dance with a woman in Madame Koto's bar:

> She drew me to her and my face pressed against her groin and an intoxicating smell staggered me like a kind of dangerous wine. The woman held my face to her and danced slowly to the music while I suffocated in an old fever that sent a radiant fire bounding through my blood... head swirling, a spasm seizing me, and still lifting, till I was almost flying, someone squirted palm-wine on my face, and I collapsed among the dancing feet in an excruciating pleasure. (272)

This sounds rather as if the boy is having a sexual experience. It is his ritualistic initiation into the world of adult sexuality.

Soon after this, a tremendous storm occurs as Azaro makes his way home from school, and as he staggers blindly through the devastation and observes the toll on human life and property, he comes to a house that looks rather like Madame Koto's. Azaro now has a vision that actualizes part of Madame Koto's significance and demonstrates her multifaceted ambivalence. In the vision, the figure of Madame Koto merges with that of the archetypal Ancient Mother, as she ritualistically bathes, feeds and anoints the boy. This suggests that, whatever Madame Koto might become later, she is also a kind, compassionate, benevolent mother figure who now performs services for the boy that would normally be done by his mother. This Ancient Mother also seems to be the embodiment of great fertility; 'A mighty statue in mahogany, powerful with the aroma of fertility. Her large breasts exuded a shameless libidinous potency.

A saffron-colored cloth had been worn round her gentle pregnancy' (290). There is almost a suggestion of rebirth here, of a mother taking care of a new-born child: 'She pulled out the edges of her green mosquito net and made me lie down on the great bed of her body smells. She smiled at me beyond the netting, her face veiled in green' (289). Also, the boy eventually crawls like a child and ventures into forbidden areas of the room.

However, even at this most 'passive' stage of his development, the boy becomes aware of Madame Koto's ambivalence and senses that her influence is not altogether beneficial, a very important aspect of the novel's significance. This Ancient Mother's smile is 'faintly sinister,' and she soon becomes an all-knowing wooden figure whose eyes are pitiless in their scrutiny and who seems to know the boy's destiny. The figure now coalesces with a supposedly pregnant Madame Koto, whose activities are becoming increasingly suspect. This confirms the ambivalence of Madame Koto who, later in the novel, will seem forever pregnant with three abiku children who will refuse to be born because they are aware of the world's villainy. The fact is that the boy has blundered into a mysterious and potentially evil world, rather like the world of Madame Koto, a world filled with mysterious objects and creatures like unformed beings, trapped ghosts, a captive bird, a complaining fly, a snake with its skin sloughed on a newspaper, and a turtle lying on its back. They all look like sacrificial elements, and the boy perceptively identifies them with the world of Madame Koto from which he must escape, for, far from being a true symbol of fertility, she has now become a destructive force that threatens to stifle life in favour of material prosperity. 'Then to my greatest horror, she moved – as if she were about to crush me into her pregnancy. I jumped down from her great body and fought my way through the tangle of cloth, screaming' (291). Thus, even when he seems most passive, the boy can, on awareness of danger and evil, rouse himself to great activity and fight his way through. The activities of this Ancient Mother, associated as they seem to be with the world of Madame Koto, constitute another attempt to lure Azaro back into the world of the unborn, maybe to sacrifice him to Madame Koto's deities. But by a tremendous act of will and audacity he is able to resist and fight his way out of the situation.

From now on, we see Azaro actively resisting the voices from the spirit world that would summon him back. As part of his resistance, he throws stones at the spirits who throw stones back at him and break the windows of the blind old man's house. The consequence is that Azaro's father beats him mercilessly for what he regards as a very expensive prank in the midst of their poverty. 'He thrashed me with the full energy and muscles of his great furious body. His flogging filled me with lightning flashes of pain. Every part of me burned with rawness.... He belted my feet, my neck, my back, my legs, my hands. He chastised me the way a master boxer beats an inferior sparring partner' (324). This is an important episode that teaching this novel to a Western audience must confront, for it raises issues of cultural relativity. To the Western imagination, this must seem like the worst form of child abuse. But the point must be made that many African fathers considered it their duty to physically discipline their recalcitrant children, taking very seriously the Biblical dictum 'spare the rod and spoil the child.' We must also realize that we have privileged information denied to the father because we know that it is the spirits, and not the child, who are responsible for the disasters, including the breaking of the windows, and the severe punishment therefore seems doubly unfair. But if we place ourselves in the position of the hapless father, we would see how these events must appear to a very poor couple who are at the end of their economic tether and who must now cope with one more apparently expensive prank by a difficult child.

Unfortunately, however, Azaro's father gives him this merciless thrashing at a time when the boy has consciously decided to cast his lot with the living and spurn the entreaties from his spirit companions in the world of the unborn. His father's violence looks like confirmation of his spirit companions' claim that the human world is characterized by extreme malevolence, misery and suffering, and he now makes a conscious decision for the first time to leave that world and return. He wills himself into a severe illness, refuses to eat, and refuses to be moved by his mother's weeping. One must say, however, that even now that he seems passively suffering, the boy is being quite intelligent and active. He is empowering himself to cope with the world of adults and he has deliberately chosen a strategy to punish his parents for their unfair treatment; and his discovery of his newly-found power gives him a feeling of pleasure and even of superiority as he feels himself growing in stature. He can even scoff at his father's ridiculous attempts to appear severe.

> Dad's face, large and severe, no longer frightened me. His assumption that the severity of his features gave him power over anything made him look a little comical. I punished him by retreating from the world. I tortured them both by listening with fullness of heart to the unsung melodies of spirit companions. My stomach, feeding on the diet of the other world, on the air of famine, grew bigger. I drank in the evils of history. I drank in the food of suffering that gathers in the space just above the air we breathe, just within the range of all that we see. And then I heard mother weeping. I refused to be moved. (325-6)

Azaro temporarily succumbs to the strong persuasion of his spirit companions and begins to travel on a long road with the three-headed spirit. But he is eventually saved by the love of his parents. However, one can argue that he is saved partly because he himself becomes increasingly unwilling to continue travelling with the spirit and decides to listen to the pleas of his father: 'His words offered me water and food and new breathing' (336).

The much longer first section of the novel, then, deals with Azaro's growth and the struggle to retain him in the world of human beings. He makes steady progress and grows into full humanhood. He is initiated and subject to temptation; he wrestles with death, descends to the depths of hell and is resurrected. He finally makes a commitment to stay, re-emerges reborn, more like a human being than anything else, having gained true insight during his illness into the true nature of worldly reality.

The teaching of this novel must go on to stress that in the second section of the novel the determined Azaro now gives great assistance to his father (Dad) who now assumes tremendous importance in this section as the people's champion. The allegorical significance of Dad's new boxing profession must be stressed. He is literally the champion of the people, fighting against all the forces of corruption, exploitation and evil. Reference must be made to his ritualistic illness and rebirth after every tremendous fight.

The teaching of this novel should also make reference to Madame Koto's role and the fact that in her growth and development from the ordinary owner of a palm-wine bar to a formidable entrepreneur she becomes a paradigm of development in Nigeria as a whole. Unfortunately, she also represents a prominent trend in African political and economic life; the feeling that if one cannot beat the system, it is better to join it and learn how to manipulate it. Her ambivalence must be stressed, an ambivalence that is confirmed by her identification, as Maggi Phillips has suggested, with the Yoruba female deity Oya, who is both on the side of death and the side of life (41). She also suggests the full development and representation, by an African male writer, of the female figure, particularly the female figure of dubious morality, who moves from angst to total agency, even if it is an agency that appalls some readers, and she becomes more than a match for the males. Discussion must also include the allegorical significance of the photographer, who represents the conscience of the nation, recording the people's plight in all its stark reality and refusing to gloss over inconvenient facts. It is significant that in the first pictures he takes of the compound's people, everyone looks miserable and unhappy. Yet he is pleased with the result because it is a realistic representation.

> The pictures were grained, there were dots over our faces, smudges everywhere. Dad looked as if he had a patch over one eye, Mum was blurred in both eyes, the children were like squirrels, and I resembled a rabbit. We all looked like celebrating refugees. We were cramped, and hungry, and our smiles were fixed. The room appeared to be constructed out of garbage and together we seemed a people who had never known happiness. (91)

The teaching of *The Last Harmattan* will proceed more or less along the same lines and will, if anything, be slightly more straightforward. The novel must first be discussed within the context of 'postmodernism' and then as an exercise in magical realism. As with *The Famished Road*, the relationship between the first section and the rest of the novel should be explored. In this regard, the situation in *The Last Harmattan* is the reverse of that in *The Famished Road* in that the first section, which largely contains the magical elements, is much shorter than the rest of the novel. The issue is, to what purpose does Cheney-Coker use magical elements in this largely epic or historical novel about the determination of a heroic people to be free? The answer seems to be that his intention is to present the history and mores of the people of kasila, the area in West Africa from which Fatmatta the Birdwoman originally came from and to which the settlers return. In this regard, one must make reference to an article by Patrick Bernard in the volume *Knowledge is More Than Mere Words*, who claims that Cheney-Coker marginalizes Kasila and downplays its importance by comparison with the detail with which the settlement of Malaguetta, the home of the new settlers, is presented. Let's quote him:

> People and places in Kasila mostly remain nameless with no historical specificity. *The Last Harmattan* marginalizes the history or the absence of history of Kasila, and represents Kasila as a people with no ancestors and no beginnings. If they have a beginning, then it is no historical capital. The history of Kasila becomes open to imaginative reduction, while that of Malaguetta becomes amenable to imaginative amplification. (165)

It is, of course, quite true that there is a much more thorough presentation of the story of Malaguetta, largely because this is Cheney-Coker's main concern in this novel. Nevertheless, he does, in the first one hundred pages or so, present the history, mores, aspirations of the people of Kasila, and this is intertwined with the magical. Fatmatta the Birdwoman has magical or supernatural origins, her father having been the Alusine Dunbar of the title, and her whole story is presented and intertwined with the story of Kasila, and this in turn goes much further back and is intertwined with African history and African culture. Thus we are presented not only with the ancestry of Fatmatta, with the experiences of people like Sulaiman the Nubian, Ahmed the Elephant Man, The Gold King, Njai the caravan merchant who is her father, and Mariamu her mother, but also the mores and customs of the people of Kasila. Thus we have the rituals of birth, marriage and death such as this one:

> Mariamu introduced her daughter to the extended family in the compound seven days after she was born. In keeping with tradition, she did not leave her room until a diviner came to see her, washed the child in a bath of the juice of lemon and avocado leaves, put some goat fat on the navel and rubbed a powder of burnt ore and the beak of an owl on her brow to keep witches away from her. The baby was golden in colour, and had long limbs and a mole over her right eye. Her head seemed unusually small though that was overshadowed by the evidence that she would have a rich and healthy crop of hair and that she already had eyes that were glassy and magnetic. She did not cry and, when left for a long time, she tried to put the big toe of her right foot in her mouth, which the diviner put down to her amazing powers of strength and domination in the future. (31)

It is to this end that we have, in the first section, a series of interlocking stories within stories, all of them concerned in one way or the other with the magical and all narrated in the same matter of fact way that compels belief. History is merged with the occult and the history of Fatmatta is intertwined with the history of Kasila. Kasila emerges not only as a place of mystery, but also as a repository of knowledge and learning. There are even down-to-earth historical details such as this one:

> One note of interest that caught the attention of Pedro Almerado, when he called at the Kasila coast in 1462 on his way to Cabra de Casa to begin a reactionary tyranny that was to last four hundred years, was that the inhabitants of the place did not resemble any other he had encountered since leaving Portugal. Tall, agile, dark and fearless, they were secretive and suspicious of strangers to the point of being treacherous, and possessed of a warlike character. Three hundred years earlier, they had lived under a monstrous and bloody tyranny south of the present town. A succession of bloody revolts finally won them the freedom that they cherished and were prepared to die for. (68)

After this, discussion of the Malaguettans' heroic struggle to be free can follow.

Of course, effective teaching of both novels should involve, maybe even begin with, a brief discussion of the history of Nigeria and Sierra Leone respectively, since *The Famished Road*, in its preoccupation with social comment, is concerned with Nigeria's recent political, social and economic history, and *The Last Harmattan*, is infused with the entire history of Sierra Leone.

WORKS CITED

Primary Works
Cheney-Coker, Syl. *The Last Harmattan of Alusine Dunbar*. London: Heinemann, 1990.
Clark, John Pepper. 'Abiku.' In *The Penguin Book of Modern African Poetry*, ed. Gerald Moore and Ulli Beier. London: Penguin, 1998, 251.
Fagunwa, D.O. *Ode Ninu Igbo Irunmale*. (Translated by Wole Soyinka as) *The Forest of a Thousand Demons*. London: Nelson, 1968.
Marquez, Gabriel Garcia. 'A Very Old Man With Enormous Wings.' In *The Bedford Introduction to Literature*, ed. Michael Meyer (fourth edition). Boston: Bedford/St. Martins, 1996, 233-7. (First published in *Leaf, Storm and Other Stories*, 1955).
Okri, Ben. *The Famished Road*. New York; Doubleday, 1993. (All quotations are from this edition.)
Soyinka, Wole. 'Abiku.' In *Idanre and Other Poems*. London: Methuen, 1967, 28-30.
—. *The Road*. Oxford: Oxford University Press, 1965.
—. 'Death In the Dawn.' In *Idanre and Other Poems*. London, Methuen, 1967, 10-11.
Tutuola, Amos. *The Palm-wine Drinkard*. London: Faber, 1952.

Secondary Sources
Abrams, M.H. and Geoffrey. Galt. Harpham. *A Glossary of Literary Terms*. Boston: Wadsworth Cengage Learning, 2009.
Aizenberg, Edna. '*The Famished Road*: Magical Realism and the Search for Social Equity.' *Yearbook of Comparative and General Literature* 43 (1995): 25-30.
Bernard, Patrick. 'Magical Realism and History in Cheney-Coker's *The Last Harmattan of Alusine Dunbar*'. In *Knowledge Is More Than Mere Words; A Critical Introduction to Sierra*

Leonean Literature, eds. Eustace Palmer and Abioseh Michael Porter. Trenton, NJ; Africa World Press, 2008, 153-179.

Cezaire-Thompson, Margaret. 'Beyond the Post-colonial Novel: Ben Okri's *The Famished Road* and its Abiku Traveller.' *The Journal of Commonwealth Literature* 31.2 (1996): 33-45.

Hawley, John C. 'Ben Okri's Spirit-Child: Abiku Migration and Post-modernity.' *Research in African Literatures* 26.1 (1995): 30-39.

Ogunsanwo, Olatubosun. 'Intertextuality and Post-Colonial Literature in Ben Okri's The Famished Road.' *Research in African Lite*ratures. 26.1 (1995): 40-52.

Oliva, Renato. 'Ben Okri's Shamanic Realism.' In *Coterminous Worlds: Magical Realism and Contemporary Post-Colonial Literature in English*, eds. Elsa Linguanti, Francesco Casotti, and Carmen Conciliio. Amsterdam: Rodopi, 1999, 171-196.

Palmer, Eustace. *Of War and Women, Oppression and Optimism: New Essays on the African Novel*. Trenton, NJ: Africa World Press, 2008. (Some of the points I make in this paper I have already made in my chapter on *The Famished Road* in this volume.)

Phillips, Maggi. 'Madame Koto: Grotesque Creatrix or the Paradox of Psychic Health?' In *Seriously Weird Papers on the Grotesque*, ed. Alice Mills. New York: Peter Lang, 1999, 35-49.

Ross, Jean W. 'Contemporary Authors Interview (with Ben Okri).' *Contemporary Authors* 138 (1993): 337-41.

Wright, Derek. '*Interpreting the Interspace: Ben Okri's The Famished Road.* CRNLE Review Journal 1-2 (1995): 18-30.

What has Criticism Got To Do With It? Teaching Theory & Criticism in African Literary Studies

Charles Nnolim

What has criticism got to do with literature and the arts? The answer is *everything*. Many post-graduate and upper-level undergraduate students are surprised when books recommended for the course in 'Literary Theory and Criticism' contain none of the familiar authors they encountered in their lower-level courses. Rather, strange authors and esoteric titles confront them: M.H. Abrams. *The Mirror and the Lamp;* Wellek and Warren, *Theory of Literature*, Northrop Frye, *Anatomy of Criticism. Trotsky, Literature and Revolution*; and at the upper levels even Stanley Hyman, *The Armed Vision* capped with M.H. Abrams, *A Glossary of Literary Terms*, and not to exclude Wilbur Scott's *Five Approaches to Literary Criticism.*

Literary criticism opens another window on literary studies, a window with many breathtaking vistas. Students are surprised that their amateurish answers to such a simple question as 'what is literature?' attract benign guffaws from their professors. Further simple questions like: Are you here to study literature of power or literature of knowledge' nearly always elicit the wrong answers.

An introductory course to literary theory and criticism will normally begin with basic definitions: what is literature?; what is plot?; what is character?; what is theme?; what is point of view?; and so on.

At this level students will be led to understand that there is a basic difference between the literature of power which is imaginative literature with its major genres and literature of knowledge which deals with facts and figures like accountancy, mathematics, history and geography. While the language of the literature of knowledge is expository and denotative the language of the literature of power is replete with proverbs, similes, metaphors and is mainly connotative. This is the language of short stories (oral and written) novels, poetry, and drama. These are subsumed under various headings: 'creative writing' 'or writing as art' or what the French call *belles lettres.*

The next level is to go frontal: what is literary criticism? After basic definitions the teacher will normally introduce M.H Abrams, and the four coordinates of art criticism (or the four causes) comprising:

a. the universe (mimetic theory or formal cause); b. the artist (expressive or romantic theory or efficient cause); c. the art (objective theory or material cause); and d. the audience (pragmatic or affective theory or final cause). As we expatiate on these, the lecturer may now introduce the major difference between literary theory and literary or practical criticism.

The next line of action is to discuss the functions of literature, of criticism and of the critic. In addition, major approaches to literary criticism will be discussed.

What follows now is a discussion of this study which consists more of suggestions on what should be discussed in a course like this than a full discussion of what I consider a discursive presentation

Criticism has two major approaches: first, the intrinsic approach which is mainly the domain of the 'New Critics', insists that literature should be tackled from *within*, and that the emphasis is on technique, the form of the work, its style, the linguistic exploits and craft of the author, the analysis of which leads to interpretation and appreciation. It is through the intrinsic approach that the reader can discover the harmony and unity embodied in a work of art and through which a proper interpretation of the work can be achieved. The intrinsic approach is the 'internal' approach to criticism in which irony, paradox, antithesis and figurative language are discussed in order to realize the total effect and aesthetic experience of the work. This is the formalistic approach to criticism.

Other major ways through which literary criticism can be approached, are lumped together under *extrinsic* approaches: biographical, historical, moral, psychological, sociological, ideological, (including Marxist and feminist) approaches. Each of these has its value and has enriched the various ways in which the criticism of literature can be approached.

But the teaching of the criticism of African literature would be rather hollow if we did not emphasize the uniqueness of African literature among the corpus of world literatures. This uniqueness starts with its oral base.

The Oral Base of African Literature

A new literature offers new and unique challenges to the critic, and requires a new critical approach. This is true of the oral base of African literature, the elements of which can be categorized as follows:

a) *Spoken,* involving proverbs, riddles, myths, legends, incantations.
b) *Sung,* including work songs, praise songs, elegies, dirges, war songs, birth songs, lampoons, lullabies, hunting songs.
c) *Acted*, featuring rituals, festivals, initiations, dances, observances, masquerades.

Since Pio Zirimu coined the term 'orature', critics have adopted it wherever the orality of African literature is highlighted, especially in its myth-making. Tutuola's works readily come to mind. Soyinka had also seriously engaged this aspect of African literature in *Myth and Culture in African Literature.*

Other unique aspects of African literature

The lecturer needs to draw attention to the following further features of our literatures:

Communal and collective experience
Group identity with emphasis on communal and collective group-felt experience; group solidarity showing group success or failure. This is what Charles Larson in *The Emergence of African Literature* calls 'situational' where whatever happens to the major or representative character affects the entire group that he represents as with, for example, Okonkwo in Achebe's *Things Fall Apart* and Ezeulu in *Arrow of God.* Since his fate is intertwined with that of his community, the individual is bound to identify with it.

Rural settings
The setting of early African literature is rural rather than industrial. Healing is spiritual rather than scientific, magical rather than medical, herbal rather than chemical.

Cyclical rhythms
In African literatures (and traditional societies), time is cyclical rather than linear and emphasizes a ritual measure of time in order to connect the past with the present. Birth, growth and death are observances where age-grade initiations are celebrated as ritual growth, following the seasonal recurrence of life, not the European idea of the march of civilization or progress.

Ancestor worship
African ritual observance culminates in ancestor worship surrounded with magic, juju and voodoo plus the masqueraders who represent the ancestors.

Language
The use of language in African literature is also unique. Most African literatures, since the impact of colonialism have been written in European languages. To lend African flavour to these literatures in foreign tongues, the language is twisted, bent, pidginized and vernacularized. And code-

mixing and code-switching became unmistakable aspects of the language of African literature. By these, the African personality and peculiar identity were firmly established as part of cultural affirmation.

Rural to urban settings and the colonial presence
Critics also identify the movement of African literature from pre-independence to post-independence. The setting of pre-independence works was, in the main, rural. In such works Chinua Achebe's *Things Fall Apart,* Nkem Nwankwo's *Wand of Noble Wood* and Elechi Amadi's *The Concubine* come readily to mind. Characters were in tune with their environment and any white character involved was a disruptive element (*Things Fall Apart* and *Arrow of God* are good examples). The staple elements were the use of our myth, festivals, marriage customs, divinations and superstitions. And the use of proverbs was another aspect of the narrative ingredients. In these works set in the rural environment, there may be heady and stubborn characters and iconoclasts but few outright criminals. Works set in rural environments were usually critical of the white man. These were followed by others set in urban areas, in cities often created by colonial administrations. Characters in these urban environments are rather uprooted from their rural setting, feel alienated and easily turn to criminality.

These characters, finding themselves in an artificial environment, faceless and often unemployed (we have in mind works like Ekwensi's *People of the City* and *Jagua Nana,* Achebe's *A Man of the People* and *No Longer at Ease*) become involved in politics with the added attraction of thuggery. Prostitution, the lure of night clubs, slum-living, shylock landlords, multi-national companies, civil servants and labourers are the staple elements.

Post-colonial settings
The African writer at this point turns his or her attention from criticism of colonial intruders to criticism of fellow African rulers who have made a mess of our independence from the colonial rulers. We have now works of self-appraisal, self-criticism, and self-reflection, attacking the bribery and corruption and failure of leadership.

Criticism

A new literature requires a new critical approach. The uniqueness of African literature created problems for the critic who was trying to find his or her feet. Other problems in the criticism of African literature arose from:

1. Its newness
2. The problem of appropriate language for African literature

3. The aesthetics of African literature
4. Appropriate definition of African literature
5. What critical standards to adopt (a) Indigenous? (b) Universal? (c) Western?
6. Who is the audience of African Literature?
7. What is its appropriate ideology?
8. Who should be its critic?
9. The problems of simultaneous existence between writers and their critics

A teacher of literary theory and criticism will remember to draw the attention of his students to other areas of literary criticism that will give the student a rounded outline. S/he will cover the following:

(a)   Literary movements, what we call the 'isms' of criticism; classicism, neoclassicism, romanticism, impressionism, naturalism, realism, expressionism, surrealism, formalism, Marxism, etc.

(b)   An advanced course may include a brief history of literary criticism with contributions from famous critics from the past, for example:
      i   Classical Antiquity (Aristotle, Horace, Longinus);
      ii Neo-classicism (Dryden, Pope)
      iii The Romantics (Wordsworth, Coleridge, Keats, Shelley)
      iv The Modern Period (Arnold, T.S. Eliot, I.A. Richards, Cleanth Brooks)

The teacher of literary criticism must not fail to emphasize the fact that art unaccompanied by criticism is dead art. And to round up, the teacher of literary criticism is urged to emphasize the following: the definition of criticism, the functions of criticism and the functions of the critic.

The word 'Criticism' comes from the Greek word 'Krinein': to judge, to discern. Criticism can also be defined as the art of judging or evaluating the beauties and the faults in a work of art objectively, without partiality, without the intrusion of our personal feelings, personal liking or disliking of either the work or its author. Criticism asks the questions: what is art?; what is its use?; why is it studied?; why is it created? and is it good or bad art? In other words, criticism deals with the worth or value of art, its importance, its merit, its service or use to humanity.

The functions of the critic

The critic performs social functions in relation to his or her contact with his or her chosen works of art. He or she is the one who estimates and passes judgement on the value and quality of the work of art and is a mediator between the specialist and the lay-man, between the art and its readership or audience. The critic exists to be of some use to the reader in helping the reader understand the work in question. So, the major social function of the critic is to arouse enthusiasm for the work by encouraging the reader buy and read it. The function of the critic is practical and he or she must subordinate personal, religious, social or political interest to the pursuit of truth devoid of any other selfish considerations. A sound critic must be detached.

The functions of criticism

1 To defend literature and justify its existence. Sir Philip Sidney wrote *An Apology For Poetry* in 1595 in reply to Stephen Gosson who in 1585 published the *School of Abuse* in which he asserted that drama encouraged prostitution, pick-pocketing, gambling and other tavern sins. In 1607, Samuel Daniel wrote *Defence of Rhyme* in answer to Thomas Watson who regarded poetry as a barbaric invention of the middle ages. In 1821, Shelley wrote his famous *A Defence of Poetry* in answer to Thomas Love Peacock who published *The Four Ages of Poetry*, which predicted the decline of poetry with the advancement of science and technology.

2 Criticism legislates taste and sets a standard.

3 Criticism acts as a guide to writers and exists to aid, guide and advise an author as to where he is going wrong. According to Matthew Arnold, a great critical epoch must precede an era of great creative achievement.

4 Criticism interprets, explains, explicates, and analyzes a work of art. It mediates between the specialist and the amateur, between the work and its audience.

5 Criticism protects the reader from poor or bad works and promotes and recommends good ones. It should aim to propagate, according to Arnold the best that is known and thought in existing works of art.

6 Criticism aims to demonstrate the application (in practice) of the principles of good writing and to expound the theories guiding literature in order to show the reader the processes by which literature is created and the processes by which it affects the mind, and demonstrate the principles that guide creative writing

7 Criticism serves the major function of appreciation through judicial criticism, addressing itself to such questions of values as:

a) Is the work good, i.e. is it ethical, honourable, excellent, fine, beneficial? And does it have worth and quality?

b) Is it true or is it a true representation of what it sets out to recreate, i.e. does it have verisimilitude, authenticity, accuracy, validity?

Can it stand any appropriate test?
   c) Is it beautiful, i.e does it have charm, grace, artistry, symmetry, proportion, polish, and refinement?

The above is what all art should aspire to (the good, the true, the beautiful). These are the absolute values.

SUGGESTED READING

Abrams, M.H. *The Mirror and the Lamp,* New York: W.W. Norton, 1958.
A Glossary of Literary Terms. (4th ed.). New York: Holt Rinehart and Winston, 1981.
Bate W.J. (ed.) *Criticism: The Major Tests.* New York: Harcourt, Brace and World. 1942.
Chapman, Raymond, *Linguistics and Literature: an Introduction to Literary Stylistics,* 1973.
Chinweizu, et al. *Toward the Decolonization of African Literature.* Enugu: Fourth Dimension, 1980.
Daiches, David. *Critical Approaches to Literature.* New Jersey: Prentice Hall, 1964.
Eagleton, Terry. *Marxism and Literary Criticism.* London: Methuen, 1976.
Forster, E.M. *Aspects of the Novel.* New York: Harcourt, Brace and World, 1927.
Frye, Northrop. *Anatomy of Criticism.* New Jersey: Princeton University Press. 1957.
Richards, I.A., *Principles of Literary Criticism.* London: Routledge and Kegan Paul, 1976.
Scott, Wilbur, *Five Approaches to Criticism.* New York: Collier Books, 1979.
Wellek, Rene and Austin Warren. *Theory of Literature.* New York: Harcourt, Brace and World, 1956.

Teaching African Literature in an Era of Technology: A Case Study of Coppin State University

Blessing Diala-Ogamba

Introduction

Technology is an instrument used in a variety of ways to our benefit. Technology is used in our everyday lives such as in school, at work, and at our leisure. Everybody uses one form of technology or another – from word processing to using the telephone, to teaching and taking classes online. Many professors surf the web for their research and also teach online, while students find surfing the web very exciting and informative. A lot of students are now taking online classes because of the convenience of using technology. Technology is a tool that can assist us and our students in a variety of ways, not just in school, but in other areas of life. Teaching African literature at Coppin State University Baltimore, Maryland has enabled me to teach to different modalities in order to reach the diverse students in my class, and encourage them to participate actively. This article therefore is a report based on my classroom experience in teaching African literature, the reception of African literature by my students, and how technology has enhanced the teaching and learning of African literature at Coppin State University.

African literature can be taught and learned by reading literary works, but there is a great difference when technology is used in addition to texts to enhance what is being taught and learned. Teaching African literature is exciting when students understand the background of the specific culture portrayed in the text. It is not always easy especially when students do not have any inclination as to why certain norms obtain in particular cultures. It becomes more difficult for fully online students who are not face to face (F2F) in class, to give the teacher direct feedback or have the opportunity to ask specific questions on any aspect of the text being studied. Using different aspects of technology has helped me to enhance the teaching of African literature, and has also helped students visualize what is taught, and become more creative in their analysis of literary texts. Since there are differences in learning styles, I have applied these differences using technology to meet the challenges of the diverse students in my class.

The study of literature does not focus only on a particular literary piece of work, but on a multidimensional world because a work of art can relate to other cultures and norms when analyzed. Different cultures can be compared to one another to find similarities and differences based on the content of the work studied. With this in mind, students will find out that the world is a global village. Technology therefore is a tool that helps students travel within this global village from the comfort of their homes, work places and from their schools as they search for information. In this way, they also learn more about the writer they are studying, the culture, political and socio-historical context of the literary work they are studying.

Tegrity

Tegrity is an aspect of technology used to enhance teaching and learning. It is a lecture capture system. It is a web-based software installed on a PC that enables the teacher to record lectures in or outside the classroom. Using Tegrity is very simple. The teacher teaches normally either in class (F2F), or hybrid or online. The lecture is recorded and saved on Tegrity where students can access the lecture anytime and from any device with Internet access, such as a computer or ipod. In F2F or hybrid classes, students can record their individual and group presentations, and go back to listen to the presentations and the teacher's comments at their own time. Tegrity is an application that combines digital, audio and video recording, electronic note taking, and internet to enhance teaching and learning. Because of these features, listening to lectures on Tegrity helps students correct any errors in their own note-taking and ask valid questions that will enable them to improve their comprehension and participation in class. It is most useful for revisions before a quiz or an examination. Students who are absent from class can access the lectures and take notes instead of calling the teacher to find out what they missed in class. Working adults find it beneficial because they can access the lecture at their convenience and still maintain their job schedule. Tegrity offers more choices to distance learners, and helps boost online students' help from the teacher. Tegrity delivers quality multimedia in every course especially in African literature, which helps students to visualize what is being taught. In this way, students' participation and performance are enhanced in the class. For distance learners or online students, Instructor video, annotations, and short notes on One Note, help to enhance their understanding and comprehension of the texts. Tegrity is a huge time saver for both students and faculty. It improves faculty efficiency, and reduces the need for office hours. Figure 1 shows the picture of the first screen that appears when Tegrity is used.

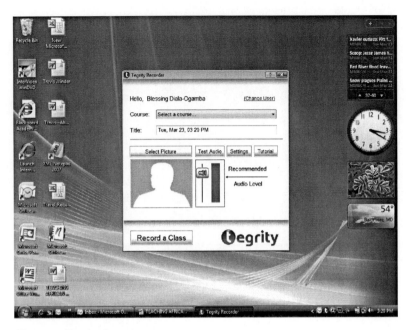

Figure 1 Tegrity homepage

How Tegrity works

To start recording on Tegrity, faculty will click on the Tegrity logo icon located in the task bar. A page appears where the instructor will locate his or her course, do an A/V test to make sure the volume is high enough, and type in the recording title before recording. There is a pause button, stop button and recording volume indicator. The instructor can pause at anytime and continue as the case may be. Tegrity has a tool bar that consists of the following: Annotations Marker and Highlighter, Drawing Object, Eraser, Switch Camera, Cursor, Annotations – Line Thickness, Lasso, Insert Blank Screen, Erase All. These features may be used as the need arises. The Blank Screen is for the instructor to write short notes. The instructor may also use another feature called One Note to write short notes for the students. The instructor uses a Marker to write on the Screen or on One Note. The notes will be transcribed immediately into typed work that will be easily identifiable for reading. If there is a mistake, the instructor can erase and rewrite as the lecture goes on. At the end of the lecture, the instructor will click to stop. Another window will open to ask if the instructor wants to end the recording. Click on Yes and the recordings will be uploaded. The instructor can preview Tegrity class recordings outside the classroom before uploading. Class recordings can be done

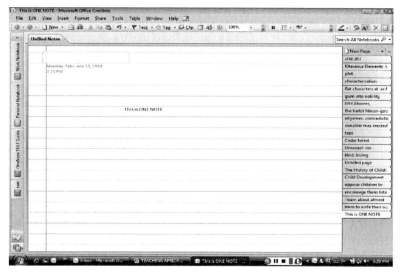

Figure 2 The task bar indicates what the instructor can use as the lecture goes on. The items on the right hand side indicate the transcription after the instructor writes with a pen.

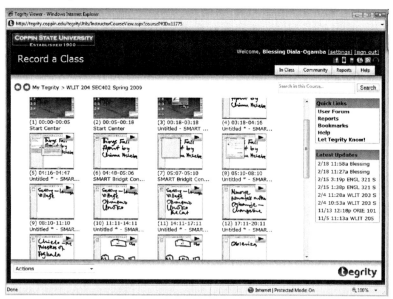

Figure 3 A Tegrity lecture on Chinua Achebe's *Things Fall Apart*. The instructor writes as the lecture goes on. Students can click on any of the items to get more clarification on what the instructor said whenever they are ready to review.

while teaching F2F or in the instructor's office, or at home before. Recordings can also be done ahead of class so students can prepare for class or online discussion. The instructor has the ability to Delete, Rename or Publish recordings for class. Once the recording is published, students can listen to Tegrity and take notes.

PowerPoint with pictures

PowerPoint is a presentation software which I also use to enhance the teaching of African Literature. Using power point helps both the teacher and students in the process of teaching and learning. Before the use of PowerPoint became popular, the only means available to the teacher for the purposes of disseminating information to students was the lecture method. The teacher sometimes enhances the lecture method by using posters in addition to lecturing, depending on the class. Sometimes, students go on excursions to different locations depending on what is being taught, and come back to listen to the teacher analyze or recreate what the students have observed. Going on an excursion to Africa from the United States of America with students will entail spending a lot of money; therefore, that is out of the question. With the help of technology, however, different innovations are used to help every student learn and practice what has been taught. In my African literature class at Coppin State University, students are encouraged to create their own PowerPoint during a group or individual presentations for class purposes. With the help of technology, they come up with more innovative ideas beyond the teacher's expectations. This method helps to foster authentic interactions and exchanges among students, and between students and teachers. From the diverse materials available on the web, students can create, and construct their presentations based on the work assigned to them. In class, the information is put together to help them understand and refine the knowledge of the literary piece they are reading.

One of the texts assigned to students in my World Literature classes is Sembene Ousmane's *God's Bits of Wood*. Before discussing this text, we have discussed literary elements and how to analyze literary works. For the group work on *God's Bits of Wood*, specific tasks were assigned to students. Students have to work individually to come up with a plan. After that, they meet in their different groups and work collaboratively, putting their plans together for class presentations. They are encouraged to use different kinds of technology available to them in order to come up with a clear and exciting presentation. At the end of each group's presentation, any inconsistency or wrong assumption is corrected, and students provide the answers to questions posed by the other groups. Selected samples of one of the innovative presentations by my students are shown in Figures 4 to 6 below. Here, the students created cartoon pictures repre-

Figure 4 Student presentation 1.

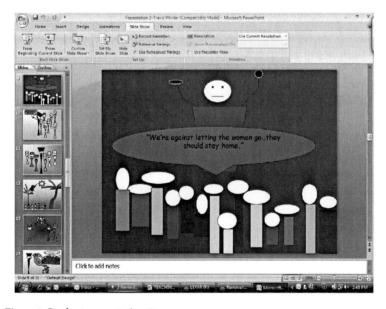

Figure 5 Student presentation 2.

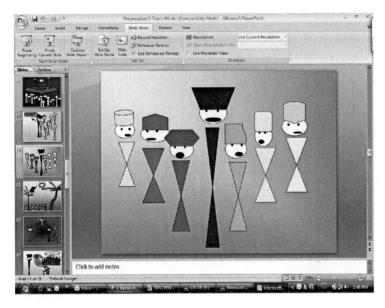

Figure 6 Student presentation 3.

senting the plot of the text assigned to them. They created their own words representing what the characters are doing in the pictures. In this way, they are free and comfortable with the presentation making the work their own as they get into the analysis of the text.

Digital storytelling

Digital Storytelling is another innovative use of technology that I incorporate in my class to enhance the teaching and learning of African Literature at Coppin State University. This method is very useful because the students will listen to the audio, and watch the video created by the teacher to enhance the understanding of the text studied. In Digital Storytelling, the best thing to do is the give the plot of the novel only. Because the students will have had the opportunity of reading the text ahead of time, the discussion of the literary elements and content of the story will follow in class (F2F), or online. The students will be able to respond to the text as discussions go on. This method will enable visual learners to understand more and participate actively in the discussions going on in class. It will also give students the opportunity to be as creative as they can be when they are doing their own presentations.

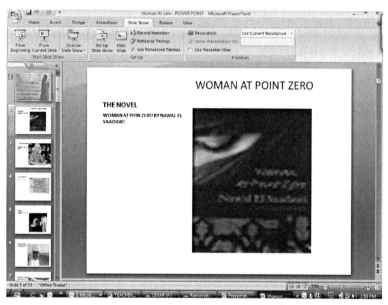

Figure 7 Creating a digital story 1.

Figure 8 Creating a digital story 2.

How digital storytelling works

The instructor creates a digital story based on the text he or she wants to teach. The story is based on the plot of the text only. The instructor looks for pictures representing the setting and the characters in the story being told. The instructor may use only pictures or add some phrases explaining what the pictures represent. The story is recorded digitally or on Tegrity. At the end, the recording with the pictures are saved so that students can play it at their own time. After listening to the story, the analysis of the text can begin in class or online depending on how the class is structured.

Using varieties of techniques provided by technology enable students to create their own stories, do a better analysis of any given literary text, and come up with creative ways of doing a group or individual presentations in class. The setting, historical, and the socio-cultural background of any given text can be included in the digital story with the help of technology. Figures 7 and 8 (left) show some pictures of the digital story I created based on Nawal El Saadawi's *Woman at Point Zero.*.

Fully online class

Fully online class is done through Blackboard which is a Course Management System. African literature can also be very well taught in fully online classes using technology. The difference here is that students will do a lot more work on their own, but they have the opportunity to use different links in the Blackboard to correspond with the teacher and their classmates in order to make sure that they are doing the correct thing. They can use the Chat Room and Discussion Board to keep pace with their assigned work. There are other links on Blackboard that they can go to, depending on what the teacher wants the class to do. Once they form the habit of reading their emails, and going to the Announcement Page to check for information, the students will not fall behind in class. At Coppin State University, most faculty members use Tegrity to enhance their fully online classes. Students appreciate this so much, and will even request the use of Tegrity if a professor does not make it part of his or her teaching tool for the class. Faculty can create hyperlinks for students instead of just using the web to gather information. Students can also create other search engines to get information for their research papers. Before classes start, the syllabus is put in the Announcement Page and also in the Document Page, so that students can start reading ahead of class in order to keep up with the class work. The due dates for assignments, discussion, quizzes and research paper are made known to the students in advance. This advanced information will help them manage their time and be on schedule. The instructor should not be rigid with due dates, because sometimes lateness of work is not always the fault of the student. Computers may break down or have other minor problems, but for the most part, the students will turn in their works on time. All the

Figure 9 What the instructor sees.

Figure 10 Announcement page of the blackboard.

information students need should be put on the Announcement Page, and they can navigate to the other parts of the Menu on the Blackboard following the instruction that is put out for them. It is also necessary to follow up announcements with emails, to avoid students coming up with excuses. If an instructor uses Tegrity in addition, students may also listen at their convenience to get additional information from the instructor which will help their understanding and comprehension of the lecture. Figure 9 is a picture of what the instructor sees and areas to navigate on Blackboard. Figure 10 is the Announcement page of the Blackboard with some announcements from the instructor.

The value of technology in teaching and learning

Technology allows students to make choices thereby empowering them and giving them the opportunity to participate actively in class. The shy students are empowered to write to their teachers expressing their opinions and asking relevant questions. Students are also encouraged to participate on the discussion board by giving their opinions on a variety of issues. Technology according to Gilberte Furstenburg "is useful not just in language learning but in the study of literature, culture, and film, as well. Ten years ago, it would have been difficult to connect words to technology and culture or technology and literature or to find synergy between those fields. Interestingly enough technology may end up being the medium that binds together the different areas of our departments, namely language, literature, culture and film" (1997: 21-5). Technology has done exactly what Furstenberg predicted, making it easy for one department to connect to another as a way to forge interdisciplinary relationship. Technology helps students to understand the linguistic, cultural, historical and socio-political and economic aspects of the literary pieces they are studying. Teaching and learning become exciting to both the faculty and students because of numerous avenues of finding sources, watching real life events of different cultures on the video, television, YouTube, as part of the class session. Relying on F2F only makes the class boring. Communication between student and teacher is easier and more convenient as students can send emails, respond on the Discussion Board or Chat Room, and get a quick reply from the teacher. Students can go to Blackboard at their convenience, so learning does not interfere with their jobs and personal activities. Technology helps both the teacher and student learn time management and become more effective. Students who are absent from class (F2F) for any reason, can listen to Tegrity for the teacher's update and take notes without calling the teacher to explain previous lectures. Technology facilitates writing, research, and helps the students to check for plagiarism before turning in their final drafts for grading. Technology is really an appropriate tool for teaching and learning anytime any day. Technology allows a learner to have choices and participate actively in a learning environment. According to G. Furstenberg: "A hypermedia environment, for instance, encourages exploratory and research-oriented inquiry and fosters the ability to observe, analyze, question, and synthesize" (21-5). Adult learners are also accommodated when technology is used to enhance teaching and learning. They do not feel shy or threatened by the younger students in the class because they have options. In fact, Madeleine Lively notes William Giezkowski's observation that older students have a favourable effect on both younger students in their classes and on the quality of instruction as teachers make adjustments according to how dynamic their classes are. Technology helps the teacher impart knowledge in a variety of ways acceptable to students of all ages. With technology students are always energized and they look forward to attending their classes wherever they may be.

Coppin State University support system

Coppin State University has a very good and efficient support system. The university supports faculty members interested in using technology by providing them with grants, PC and some stipend to start with. Faculty have the opportunity of being trained by the best technology specialists at Coppin. Training and using technology is not compulsory, but a lot more faculty are using the technology now in teaching and learning especially with outbreak of the H1N1 virus. The Adjunct faculty members are all given PCs to help them in their classes and in the case of an out break of disease, they can teach from home. Coppin gives faculty the basic training that starts with how to upload syllabus online and how to record on Tegrity, to more advanced trainings. The training level required by each faculty depends on the faculty. Different kinds of workshops are organized by the IT division. Conferences on Teaching and Learning with Technology are organized by the Technology division of the University, and faculty members are encouraged to present their works and findings at these conferences. Coppin State University also encourages faculty to present at Technology Conferences anywhere in the world. Faculty are given the opportunity to play direct roles in making decisions on the type of technology the University can purchase to enhance teaching and learning with technology. Faculty participation is very important because they are the people who will use the technology directly to reach the students.

Conclusion

Until recently, we did not know that technology would be as much a part of our lives as it has been. We use it in different forms in our daily lives – at school, home, for leisure and at our work places. Almost everybody uses technology in one form or another, but a lot of progress has been made in terms of using a variety of soft ware in teaching and learning. Many faculty members find it beneficial to teach online and surf the web for their research. Students too find surfing the web exciting, therefore they register for online classes for their convenience. Faculty should not be afraid of using technology because we need to meet the students where they are if we want to keep them and keep our jobs. Different subjects including African literature can be taught using technology. We therefore have to continue to learn different ways to integrate technology into our teaching and learning, and also encourage students to use technology, especially older students, by connecting them with help desk numbers to call, and giving them enough time to practice on their own in the lab or at home. With technology, students can learn more about the culture, norms, history and socio-economic and political context of African literary pieces they are studying, without having to travel to the African continent.

WORKS CITED

Achebe, Chinua. *Things Fall Apart*. London: Heinemann, 1958.
El Sadaawi, Nawal. *Woman at Point Zero*. London: Zed Books, 2007.
Furstenburg, Gilbert. 'Teaching with Technology: What is at Stake?' *ADFL Bulletin* 28, no.3 (Spring 1997): 21-5
Lively, Madeleine. 'The Changing Demographics of the Traditional Student: Making Our Classroom Relevant for the New Generation'. *ADFL Bulletin*. 28, no 3 (Spring 1997): 32-6.
Ousmane, Sembene. *God's Bits of Wood*. Oxford: Heinemann, 1960.

Teaching African Literature Online in America: A University of Michigan-Flint Initiative

Patricia Thornton Emenyonu

African literature courses have been taught at the University of Michigan-Flint for nearly thirty years. The Department of Africana Studies was established in 1974 as a Program with multi-disciplinary offerings in history, political science, sociology, economics, music, art, drama and literature. It became a department in 1999. Currently, 65 Africana courses from introductory to upper level are listed in the catalogue. Students can major or minor in Africana Studies, and there is also a certificate program. However, for the past seven years, enrolment in the African literature classes has fluctuated causing course cancellations over several semesters. About three years ago, the Department decided to embark on a new approach to learning, and several professors undertook to transform traditional face-to-face classes to online. The result is a most remarkable success story.

As Draves (2002) has pointed out:

> There are some immediate and practical reasons why we're teaching online these days. The cost of travel, time involved, need for quick updates and information, offerings at only one day and time, and only one location, are a few limitations of face-to-face classrooms...Our society is moving rapidly from an industrial or manufacturing-based society into an information or knowledge economy. Online learning responds to an information or knowledge-based economy. (153)

Experts in the field of online teaching predict that in the twenty-first century, 50 per cent of all learning and education will be online. (5) They go further to say, 'The education revolution will have as profound and as far-reaching an effect upon the world as the invention of printing. Not only will it affect where we learn, it also will influence how we learn and what we learn.' (Celente, 1997, in Draves, 5)

Where our students learned was initially in the classroom even if that was not convenient or had to be navigated around work schedules and child care responsibilities. The University of Michigan-Flint is part of the University of Michigan system of three campuses: Ann Arbor, Dearborn and Flint. Unlike Ann Arbor, our campus has a student population which is still predominantly nontraditional. Nontraditional students are defined as 'working adults returning to school or students who are unable to attend classes on campus for other reasons.' (Palloff and Pratt, 3) In the case of Flint, the reasons our students were commuters (besides the fact that we had no dormitories until recently) included factors such as economic hardship which meant many of them had to support families by working full time or having multiple part-time jobs while taking classes. They no longer had opportunities to work in the auto industry which, just a decade ago, had hired assembly line workers right out of high school for excellent wages with benefits. Allowing our students to learn from home or work had many advantages. They could learn during their peak learning time and not be forced to take a class that met at a particular time on a particular day/s. Students could learn at their own speed. Fast or slow is possible in the same class. Students could interact more with their lecturer.

The very definitions of 'education' and 'learning' have changed. Brooks and Brooks (1993) explained that 'Current constructivist theory holds that students, through their interaction with one another, the instructor, and their environment, create knowledge and meaning.' (quoted in Palloff and Pratt, 3)

How could we design our online African literature courses so that this interaction between students and between students and teacher could be optimized? We were obliged to use the Blackboard software as the vehicle for this course construction. When students log on to Blackboard they have a menu that lists ten areas they can access:

- Announcements
- Course Information
- Staff Information
- Course Documents
- Assignments
- Discussion Board
- Communication
- External Links
- My Grades
- Tools

'**Announcements**' is the Home Page for the course. It is what students see when they log on to the course. Here the lecturer can inform students of graded assignments that have been posted or new events that could be an opportunity for extra credit. If Discussion Feedback has been posted, a link from the Announcements page can be created so they can go directly to the area to read the feedback. When posting an announcement, it can be sent to all students as an email as well by checking a box when creating the announcement. If a test is available, an announcement can also be created to remind students that it is ready. It is the current affairs site for the lecturer to keep students informed of due dates for tests, assignments, projects, etc. and to alert them when grades or comments have been posted.

'**Course Information**', the second area, is where students will find a copy of the syllabus. I like to allow students a certain amount of choice in what they must read. In AFA 318, *Women Writers of the African World,* for example, I require students to read four novels. For the second novel, they may choose between two similar books written by two different women whose protagonists were part of Islamic communities. Topics for discussion covering marriage and treatment of women under Islam could be answered using examples from either of the texts. Students would also be given choice in the selection of their fourth novel which would be part of a final project and would be chosen individually by each student and approved by the teacher. Students' interests and backgrounds are not the same. By providing an element of choice in the selection of what is read, students may feel more self-motivated to complete assignments and read the material provided to introduce a theoretical basis for interpretations and analyses of works written by African authors whose settings, protagonists' names and traits, and story lines may be unfamiliar to American students. It helps to establish a sense of trust and mutual respect. If the teacher has done a good job in the initial selection of novels, short stories, poems, or drama, and is able to draw connections from the known to the unknown in terms of themes, settings, characterization, style, figurative language and other literary devices, then the students will be active participants in the exploration of African literature and its relationship to the Diaspora especially the United States.

Taking into account different learning styles, the syllabus includes assessment that is varied and based on a point system. I like to use a positive system of 1000 points possible with no more than 10 per cent for extra credit above that total. That allows me to award more points for each assignment. For example, if a paper is worth 100 points it seems more significant than if it were worth only 10 points if I had a 100 point system. About a fourth of the points possible would be assigned to the weekly discussion participation; another fourth to tests over each required novel read in class. The type and form of each book quiz would be constant so that students could expect a consistent format and type of question and learn from their mistakes or shortcomings from first quiz to last. The third quarter would come from two short papers one written before the mid-semester period and the second after. The final quarter would be the Final Project – the self-selected novel and report using power point on an author of the student's choice.

'**Staff Information**' is where I place my biographical and professional data. I like to indicate through this brief history of my life and academic qualifications just why I feel ready, eager and able to teach this particular course. The write-up also permits me to set the tone for the course showing that personal information can be shared in a safe environment. There is also a picture of me so they have a sense of who I am.

'**Course Documents**' is a place to post weekly lectures and to scan in articles, chapters from books, poems, excerpts from novels or plays, pictures and anything that would help engage the students in the required reading or provide supplementary information to fill in or expand on ideas based on the assigned novel. Because of copyright rules, I must be careful to scan in poems, short stories, chapters from books, or articles from journals or critical collections which are within the number of pages allowed for academic purposes to share in the classroom. There are some materials that are out of print or hard to locate. By scanning them in under Documents, students are saved the expense and time it would take to try to locate them on their own. See Appendix A for an example.

'**Assignments**' is the first place students should go after logging on and checking for any new announcements. This area is organized week by week. I like to create folders which I color code alternating red and green, for example. The title will be 'Week One' with the date of the Monday for that week appearing next to the title. In the space below the title, I may put the title of the book we are reading that week or a theme we are discussing from that book. Inside the weekly folder will be a standard list of assignments: Lecture, Reading, Discussion Board, and External Links. If there is a paper due, another written assignment or test, then that would be listed as well. These files will also be colour coded so that the lecture is one colour, discussion board another, and so on. I never just assign a number of pages to be read. I try to summarize something that happens in this section of the book and ask a question or ask them to look out for an event, person, place, or idea in order to guide the reading and give it some purpose. See Appendix B for an example.

The '**Discussion Board**' is one of the most important areas because it is where I take attendance in a way. Students are required to participate in discussions every week. By requiring that students participate in weekly discussions by posting their own comments to questions or statements developed by the lecturer to stimulate critical thinking and by responding to at least two other students' posts each week, a learning community gradually develops over the course of the first few weeks of class. I like to stay neutral while the students discuss among themselves and at the end of the week select pertinent quotes from students' comments and create a commentary feedback that supports good thinking, reinforces thoughtful analysis, and presents alternative views or opinions for students to consider. Individual feedback on every post could be very time consuming, but a group feedback that highlights the best points and analyses and brings new ideas to the table can provide excellent 'teachable moments' while thoughts are still fresh. See Appendix C for an example.

The first week's discussion is always an introduction of self. My profile is placed under 'Staff Information', so they have some idea of who I am. I do have students fill out an Information Sheet which gives me a phone contact and provides some background on the student such as whether this is his/her first Africana Studies class, what the student's major and minor are, what organizations s/he belongs to, what interests s/he may have, whether they are married or have children, whether they work, etc. But this information is confidential and for the teacher's eyes only. So students need to introduce themselves to the class and begin to listen to each other. Some students may have taken other classes with students in this class and they acknowledge this connection. Some may have a common family situation or ethnic connection. For some the style of communication gives a clue to their personality. I often feel that I get to know my students better in an online class than in a face-to-face class. Everyone 'talks' through their written comments and posts. There is no sitting at the back of the room in silence.

'**External Links**' provides an area to share websites that can give great background information and visual depth to topics. There are numerous internet sources to supplement the texts I use. Some are author sites which give biographical information and list other published works. Some are interview sites which provide live footage of the author speaking with a reporter. Some give background information about the country the creative work is set in. Some provide media information for African newspapers. Some are university sites that provide a variety of listings which may include lesson plans for teaching an African novel, author, or theme. I have found Boston University's African Tutorial a good general introduction to the continent for beginning students. Some are links to organizations that feature Africa – the National Geographic Society, PBS, or former President Carter's The Carter Center which focuses on health and peace initiatives, the Bill and Melinda Gates Foundation, or former President Clinton's Global Initiatives.

'**My Grades**' provides students with an up-to-date record of how they are doing in the class. It should be current and provide constant and immediate feedback for graded assignments, tests and any other form of assessment. When a test is created in Blackboard, it may be scored online and the points automatically recorded under the Grade Center. In addition to scoring test questions, there is a box to record comments for each section of the test. Where a simple acknowledgement of a right response is all that is required, such as, 'Full credit', the system allows you to copy and paste from test to test to save time. Students do not have to wait for the next class for tests/papers to be returned. They are available as soon as they are graded. Feedback is fast and may include examples of the best answers from the class as a model.

'**Tools**' enables me to create a unique template for my home page. I like to have a banner that reflects the course content. I want the tabs and menu to be in colours that match and compliment the banner. Students should feel a sense of Africa as if they are entering a special world through a technological link to the continent. See course banner under Appendix D.

Blackboard provides the format to organize the African literature course online. It is the lecturer who utilizes the space to provide students with the best learning experience possible. Because of the nature of the content, African literature classes may attract African-American students in larger numbers than other American literature or British literature courses. It is important to be aware of best pedagogical practices for reaching all students especially culturally diverse students. The Fall 2009 issue of *Teaching Tolerance* magazine is devoted to 'Teaching Diverse Students'. The African literature classroom should be a space where teachers and students can talk about difference. As Jenee Darden's article 'Talking Race' indicates, 'The most significant educational challenge facing the United States is the tragically low academic achievement of many students of color' (52). She further provides a solution to this problem, 'The Teaching Diverse Students Initiative (TDSi) helps educators meet this challenge by providing them with research-based resources for improving the teaching of racially and ethnically diverse students' (52).

So what would culturally relevant pedagogy look like? Ana Maria Villegas, Tamara Lucas, Beverly Armento and Jacqueline Jordan Irvine have identified 15 culturally relevant instructional behaviours. Most of these can be applied in an online course as easily as in a traditional face-to-face classroom:

- Involving students in the construction of knowledge
- Building on students' interests and linguistic resources
- Tapping community and home resources
- Helping students examine the curriculum from multiple perspectives
- Using a variety of valid assessment practices that promote learning
- Using examples and analogies from students' lives
- Instituting a positive classroom climate
- Developing positive relationships with parents and community
- Understanding students' cultural knowledge and experiences and selecting appropriate instructional materials
- Helping students find meaning and purpose in what is to be learned
- Using interactive and constructivist teaching strategies
- Preparing students to effect changes in society
- Helping learners construct meaning by organizing, elaborating and representing knowledge in their own way
- Using primary sources of data and manipulative materials
- Aligning assessment with teaching through activities like teacher observations, student exhibitions and portfolios.

In addition to this list, TDSi educators fully endorse the belief that good educational practices are not about lowering high expectations. Course content should be rigorous and students held accountable for learning it. Teachers in our public schools need to be encouraged to question the curriculum and the pedagogy. Teachers cannot be expected to value and espouse multicultural texts and content after attending superficial, one-day teacher workshops. Students need more than a focus on international festivals and once-a-year programs. As Darden has so aptly put it, 'Food, folklore and festivals are not the same as an analysis of race in America.' And so the courses offered in the Africana Studies Department at University of Michigan-Flint attempt to provide content that has long been omitted from the curriculum of schools at all levels. We are located in a city that has a large black population with high schools that are approximately 90 per cent black with drop-out rates that exceed 50 per cent. Minority students entering our literature classes feel like they have lived in a desert and suddenly found an oasis. Those who come out of curiosity, leave believing that Africa may not be so different from the United States. Or at least that customs that they find 'strange' such as polygamy or excision have a rational basis in an agrarian, patriarchal culture.

Using *Women Writers of the African World* (AFA 318) as an example, let's examine ways that course readings can stimulate interest in Nigeria/Senegal/Egypt/South Africa or other parts of Africa that authors depict without creating stereotypes and glib impressions of patriarchy. Since the course focuses on female authors and attracts large numbers of female students, definitions of feminism and womanism are studied first before embarking on *The Joys of Motherhood* by Nigerian author Buchi Emecheta, our first required novel. American and African scholars' papers are read and the Discussion Board asks students to consider how feminism in the US has affected them. 'Has the Feminist Movement made life in the U.S. better? Why or why not?' Then as they read Emecheta's novel, they also compare their personal experiences with those of the protagonist: 'And they all agreed that *a woman without a child* for her husband was *a failed woman.*' p. 62. How do you react to such statements? Do women in the US consider themselves failures if they have no children? The Discussion Board provides a forum for opinions, even prejudices, personal stories, interpretations, analyses, and commentaries to be voiced which connect what students are reading with their lives and experiences and each other. A deeper sense of the themes and stories emerges through this cyber talk even when we never see each others' faces. Our words paint a picture and create a sense of purpose and culturally responsive participation.

Selections to introduce students to Africa are also carefully chosen. An article '*I Didn't Know There Were Cities In Africa: Challenging Children's – and Adults' – Misperceptions about the African Continent*' by Brenda Randolph and Elizabeth DeMulder help students to consider issues of primitivity/barbarity or romantic/naturalistic views of Africa. 'The portrayal of Africa in Western media and children's books continues to feed a belief in white superiority and the need for Africans (Blacks) to be saved or feared.' (39) Colleagues in other Departments at the University of Michigan-Flint seem to be surprised that there are Nobel-winning authors from the African continent. They might well wonder, 'I Didn't Know There were Good Novels Written in English (not translation) Coming from Africa.' As African authors through the various African literature courses become familiar to the campus community; as their novels/works sit side by side with American and British and other writers on the shelves of the University Bookstore; as faculty hear students discussing or comparing African texts to ones read in American literature classes – we are making a difference. Our presence is being felt even beyond the campus.

Has online made a difference for African literature at the University of Michigan-Flint? Using three courses as examples, the difference is clear. When AFA 206, *Survey of African Literature*, was last taught face-to-face over two years ago, enrollment struggled to reach university acceptable levels and was finally allowed to hold with 7 students. When first introduced online in the Winter 2009 semester, enrollment jumped to 30 (the limit) with a wait list. It has continued to be taught Fall and Winter semesters ever since with student numbers between 25 and 30 consistently. Likewise AFA 207, *Modern African Drama and Poetry*, had 10 students maximum when taught face-to-face and rose to 30 students when online with a waitlist. As for AFA 318, *Women Writers of the African World*, it sputtered along with 12 students when last taught face-to-face, but when converted to online, it has been offered three semesters consecutively for the past three years with class size between 25 and 30 students each semester.

Although online courses were geared to non-traditional students, increasing numbers of campus-based students are equally attracted to online courses. We are also able to reach a much wider audience even attracting students from out of state and out of the country.

WORKS CITED

Darden, Jenee. 'Talking Race: Making a space where teachers can talk about difference.' In *Teaching Tolerance*, Fall 2009, pp. 49-53.

Draves, William A. (2002). *Teaching Online*. River Falls, WI: LERN

Emecheta, Buchi. (1979). *The Joys of Motherhood*. London: Allison & Busby.

Irvine, Jacqueline Jordan. 'Relevant Beyond the Basics.' In *Teaching Tolerance*, Fall 2009, pp. 41-4.

Palloff, Renea M. & Keith Pratt. (2001). *Lessons from the Cyberspace Classroom: The realities of online teaching*. San Francisco: Jossey-Bass.

Randolph, Brenda & Elizabeth DeMulder. 'I Didn't Know There were Cities in Africa!' *Teaching Tolerance*, Fall 2008, pp 36-43.

White, Ken W. & Bob H. Weight. (2000). *The Online Teaching Guide: A handbook of attitudes, strategies, and techniques for the virtual classroom.* Boston: Allyn and Bacon.

APPENDICES

Appendix A

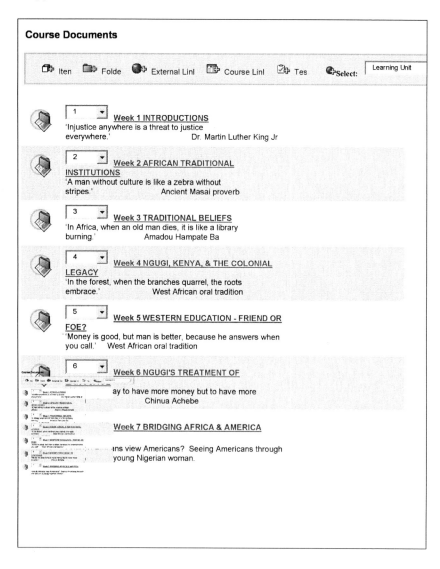

Course Documents

Iten   Folde   External Linl   Course Linl   Tes   Select: Learning Unit

1   Week 1 INTRODUCTIONS
'Injustice anywhere is a threat to justice everywhere.'   Dr. Martin Luther King Jr

2   Week 2 AFRICAN TRADITIONAL INSTITUTIONS
'A man without culture is like a zebra without stripes.'   Ancient Masai proverb

3   Week 3 TRADITIONAL BELIEFS
'In Africa, when an old man dies, it is like a library burning.'   Amadou Hampate Ba

4   Week 4 NGUGI, KENYA, & THE COLONIAL LEGACY
'In the forest, when the branches quarrel, the roots embrace.'   West African oral tradition

5   Week 5 WESTERN EDUCATION - FRIEND OR FOE?
'Money is good, but man is better, because he answers when you call.'   West African oral tradition

6   Week 6 NGUGI'S TREATMENT OF
ay to have more money but to have more   Chinua Achebe

Week 7 BRIDGING AFRICA & AMERICA
ans view Americans? Seeing Americans through young Nigerian woman.

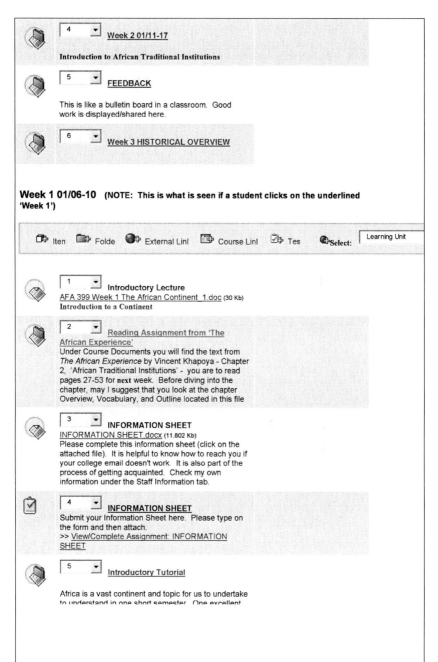

4 ▼ <u>Week 2 01/11-17</u>

Introduction to African Traditional Institutions

5 ▼ <u>FEEDBACK</u>

This is like a bulletin board in a classroom. Good work is displayed/shared here.

6 ▼ <u>Week 3 HISTORICAL OVERVIEW</u>

Week 1 01/06-10 (NOTE: This is what is seen if a student clicks on the underlined 'Week 1')

☐⁺ Iten   ☐⁺ Folde   ●⁺ External Linl   ☐⁺ Course Linl   ☑⁺ Tes   ⊕ Select: [Learning Unit

1 ▼ Introductory Lecture
<u>AFA 399 Week 1 The African Continent_1.doc</u> (30 Kb)
Introduction to a Continent

2 ▼ <u>Reading Assignment from 'The African Experience'</u>
Under Course Documents you will find the text from *The African Experience* by Vincent Khapoya - Chapter 2, 'African Traditional Institutions' - you are to read pages 27-53 for next week. Before diving into the chapter, may I suggest that you look at the chapter Overview, Vocabulary, and Outline located in this file

3 ▼ INFORMATION SHEET
<u>INFORMATION SHEET.docx</u> (11.802 Kb)
Please complete this information sheet (click on the attached file). It is helpful to know how to reach you if your college email doesn't work. It is also part of the process of getting acquainted. Check my own information under the Staff Information tab.

4 ▼ <u>INFORMATION SHEET</u>
Submit your Information Sheet here. Please type on the form and then attach.
>> <u>View/Complete Assignment: INFORMATION SHEET</u>

5 ▼ Introductory Tutorial

Africa is a vast continent and topic for us to undertake to understand in one short semester. One excellent

Appendix B

Assignments   (NOTE: This is what students will see when they open this tab)

 Iten   Folde   External Linl   Course Linl   Tes   Select: Learning U

---

 1 ▼   MAP OF AFRICA QUIZ

Because of problems designing a map quiz for BlackBoard, I am asking you to follow the link below and take the quiz.

http://www.ilike2learn.com/ilike2learn/africa.html

When you click on the link, you will see in bright red ' | Under which will be in red letters 'Africa Map Quiz'. Each quiz is unique. The name of a country appears on the right and the mapis to the left. You must click on the country that matches the name.

You will need to copy your results and email them to me so that I can record them in the Grade Center. I will have to trust you on this one. I will use the percentage of correct answers to convert to the 50 points.

 2 ▼   **GENERAL EXPECTATIONS**

Check your UMF e-mail *every 48 hours* and especially after a deadline, in case there is a problem with your assignment and I need to reach you. I will send out announcements weekly and more often if need be. The UMF e-mail is the only e-mail address the University or Blackboard recognizes, so it will be my primary means of contacting you. **NOTE:** You can not forward your University e-mail to another account, so you **must** check your UMF account.

Further Expectations are to be read in the file attached.

 3 ▼   Week 1 01/06-10

Misconceptions of Africa & Social Institutions

Each week as you open your Assignments Folder you should expect to find possible links under your **Documents Tab** where the Lecture for the week is kept; the **Reading Assignment** for the week is kept; mention of the **External Link** you are to explore (you will compare any 3 of these sites by the end of the semester); and any **Written Assignment** which will be due or started/drafted - not every week will have a written assignment. Participation in the **Discussion**

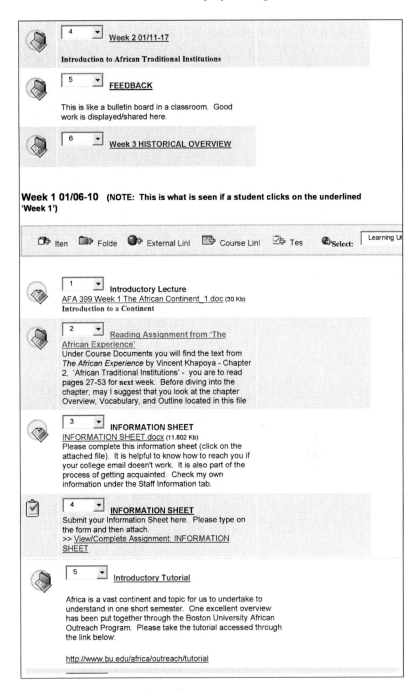

4 ▾   Week 2 01/11-17

Introduction to African Traditional Institutions

5 ▾   FEEDBACK

This is like a bulletin board in a classroom. Good work is displayed/shared here.

6 ▾   Week 3 HISTORICAL OVERVIEW

Week 1 01/06-10   (NOTE: This is what is seen if a student clicks on the underlined 'Week 1')

▥ Iten   ▥ Folde   ▥ External Linl   ▥ Course Linl   ▥ Tes   ▥ Select: [Learning U

1 ▾   Introductory Lecture
AFA 399 Week 1 The African Continent_1.doc (30 Kb)
Introduction to a Continent

2 ▾   Reading Assignment from 'The African Experience'
Under Course Documents you will find the text from *The African Experience* by Vincent Khapoya - Chapter 2, 'African Traditional Institutions' - you are to read pages 27-53 for **next** week. Before diving into the chapter, may I suggest that you look at the chapter Overview, Vocabulary, and Outline located in this file

3 ▾   INFORMATION SHEET
INFORMATION SHEET.docx (11.802 Kb)
Please complete this information sheet (click on the attached file). It is helpful to know how to reach you if your college email doesn't work. It is also part of the process of getting acquainted. Check my own information under the Staff Information tab.

4 ▾   INFORMATION SHEET
Submit your Information Sheet here. Please type on the form and then attach.
>> View/Complete Assignment: INFORMATION SHEET

5 ▾   Introductory Tutorial

Africa is a vast continent and topic for us to undertake to understand in one short semester. One excellent overview has been put together through the Boston University African Outreach Program. Please take the tutorial accessed through the link below:

http://www.bu.edu/africa/outreach/tutorial

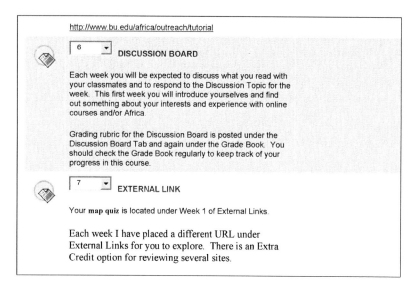

http://www.bu.edu/africa/outreach/tutorial

DISCUSSION BOARD

Each week you will be expected to discuss what you read with your classmates and to respond to the Discussion Topic for the week. This first week you will introduce yourselves and find out something about your interests and experience with online courses and/or Africa.

Grading rubric for the Discussion Board is posted under the Discussion Board Tab and again under the Grade Book. You should check the Grade Book regularly to keep track of your progress in this course.

EXTERNAL LINK

Your **map quiz** is located under Week 1 of External Links.

Each week I have placed a different URL under External Links for you to explore. There is an Extra Credit option for reviewing several sites.

Appendix C Example of the Feedback for Discussion #3 in 'Africana Studies for Teachers'

DB 3 FEEDBACK AFA 399/599

On p. 72 of *The River Between* Waiyaki has become the pride of the people of Kameno and they had started calling him the champion of the tribe's way of life, yet he still had doubts about himself. 'Yet he sometimes wondered. Was the education he was trying to spread in the ridges not a contamination?'

What do you think? (My comments follow and then student responses)

The words we use to describe people (educated, knowledgeable, illiterate, ignorant, traditional, tribal, modern) are 'loaded' terms. Illiteracy has to do with being able to read and write. A literate person used to be defined as being able to read at a 4th grade level. It is no longer considered adequate and the bar has been raised to say the 6th grade level. But then would you call a person 'educated' simply because they can read and write? Is a person who can't read or write ignorant? The more we study language, the more we realize that it is so important as a vehicle for understanding a people's culture. As a language becomes extinct, as many are all over the world, a whole branch of knowledge dies. People may be very skilled at 'reading' the earth or at 'reading' the human body. Some doctors in Nigeria quickly agree that traditional bone healers are often far better at setting broken arms or legs than they are in hospitals. Words can be pejorative. They can carry a lot of unwelcome baggage. One such word is tribe.

When we identify a person as coming from a particular 'tribe' it is like we have put a value judgment in place that s/he comes from a group of people who are primitive/savage/uneducated. If you want to refer to someone from a particular ethnic group, then use the name of his/her language or ethnicity. (Kikuyu, Igbo, Yoruba, Fante…)

I just attended a program that was sponsored by people who are committed to ensuring Social Justice for farmers in Ethiopia. They are concerned that 'well-meaning', wealthy philanthropists such as Bill & Melinda Gates are pushing for 'development' in Ethiopia through the use of 'modern' (better) technology and genetically modified seeds (their Foundation has links with the largest of the seed companies, Monsanto?). The so-called Green Revolution has produced some disastrous results in such countries as India because of assumptions that big and technical is better. Money is power. With power comes control. And that control includes the media/communication. I think several of you raised important questions which is why we offer a course such as this. I would hope that you pursue these questions in relation to a country in Africa that you have chosen to learn more about in your Projects.

Tenicka   there is a difference, and I hope we all get that, between being sheltered or segregated and being ignorant. I don't think that you were calling the Kikuyu people of indigenous beliefs ignorant but I think that we need to be careful when we say that 'he wanted to give his people the opportunity to learn.' Self-segregation for preservation sake for many indigenous people is a reaction to the fear of cultural extinction. One can learn about another way, but the changing shouldn't be forced upon the indigenous but rather on the colonizers. This is an issue of access, privilege and power- being genuinely educated is a small part of what is really going on here. The intentions and implications are far less philanthropic than you led to. Let us remember that this is a piece of historical fiction. There are real Kikuya peoples in Kenya who underwent similar circumstances and I would argue that they are not more well off than their predecessors.

Tammy   Robert Fulghum, author of 'All I really Need to Know I Learned in Kindergarten', wrote:

'I believe that imagination is stronger than knowledge —
that myth is more potent than history.
I believe that dreams are more powerful than facts —
That hope always triumphs over experience —
That laughter is the only cure for grief.
And I believe that love is stronger than death.'

I think that having knowledge goes beyond just the textbook education one is exposed to. If you contemplate your own education you have to admit that educators do have the influence to 'contaminate', or strongly influence, how we interpret certain things we encounter that fall within the realm of their educational expertise and this influence, or contamination, for better or for worse, can remain with us for a long time and maybe even forever. It is to infer that any of us our vulnerable or naive in allowing such individuals seated in these positions of authority to influence us, we actively allow this to occur for a multitude of reasons. Many of us are on our own paths of self discovery and are seeking that one bit of knowledge that already agrees with our own way of reasoning and in the process of learning from these individuals we allow more than just that particular lesson to leave a lasting impression on us. Some times we learn the lesson and we take with us some thing more from that mentor that enlighten our thinking. I think that it is only when we find our own intellectual voices and we are learned enough to be at par with our mentors that we can truly sit and contemplate exactly to what extreme we were influenced (or contaminated) and assess whether the path that thinking toke us down was conducive to our own intellectual nourishment or not.

Knowledge is not just knowing what to do but more importantly it is knowing what not to do (can't remember the author of the quote, just wanted to mention I could not come up with something this wise). The fact that Waiyaki is wise enough to be burdened with whether what he spreads is actually a 'contamination' to his Kameno brethren indicates that he probably possessed or had already had exposure to knowledge that was nourishing for his own intellectual well being and that the knowledge he had been exposed to by outsiders was probably something that he could have even lived without.

In 2008 a tribe of primitive people who had never had contact with modern people was discovered in the Amazon near the Brazilian-Peruvian borders. The picture I recall is of tribes men taking aim with their bow and arrows as a research prop plane flew over their grounds. They survived for ages without 'our' modern form of knowledge. Apparently our knowledge, or in Waiyaki's case the knowledge he brought to the Kamenos, might not be the necessity some would think it may, or rather should, be.

Richard   But let me ask you this question, does a multiracial person embrace one of their cultures or all of them?   It depends on the family or in Waiyaki's situation the tribe.

Angela   Change is painful but when you come into an area and tell those people they are wrong for the way they live, that is contamination when you try to teach them the 'proper way' according to you and your people. Our education is superior?   Maybe the tribes education was superior to the white man? What are the guidelines for being superior? Being white? Coming from Europe? Maybe non circumcision was barbaric to the tribe. Who is to say WHAT type of education is the best kind? The white man? The tribe?

Stefanie if he was promoting the white man's religions and traditions that would have been contamination. It is almost like a missionary from the inside. <u>Communication is always the key to knowledge</u>, and I think he broke (or tried to break) that communication barrier between the white man and the tribe in an effort to help them reach a sense of understanding of each other......with education came awareness of their colonizers and their surroundings, and this brought contamination. They were now contaminated by the west and their commercialism, their wars, and their ways.

Appendix D Sample Banner seen on 'Home Page' of the course:

Appendix E

AFA/CPL/WGS 318: WOMEN WRITERS OF THE AFRICAN WORLD

Instructor: Pat Emenyonu **Winter 2010 online**
Office: 320B French Hall   **Office Hours:** 3:00- 4:00 pm W R/appt.
Email: patemen@umflint.edu **Phone:** 762-3474

Required Texts:
1. *The Joys of Motherhood*, Buchi Emecheta
2. *So Long a Letter,* Mariama Ba **OR**
   Woman at Point Zero, Nawal El Saadawi
3. *The Color Purple*, Alice Walker
4. **Novel of your choice** for Final Project – African American, Caribbean or African author

Additional readings will be posted under the Documents Tab
- *The Feminist Mystique*, Chapter 1
- C-SPAN American Writers II: Betty Friedan. http://www.american-writers.org/writers/friedan.asp
- National Organization for Women http://www.now.org/
- Interview: Betty Friedan www.pbs.org/fmc/interviews/friedan. htm
- Excerpt from bell hooks *Feminism is for Everyone*
- 3 articles from *Feminism and Sisterhood,* Obioma Nnaemeka (Ed.)
  a. Angela Miles, 'North American Feminisms/Global Feminisms – Contradictory or Complementary?'
  b. 'Zulu Sofola, 'Feminism and African Womanhood.'
  c. Flora Nwapa, 'Women and Creative Writing in Africa.'
- *Crossing Water: Contemporary Poetry of the English-Speaking Caribbean* (1992) edited by Anthony Kellman.
  a. Lorna Goodison's (Jamaica) 'Guinea Woman'
  b. Claire Harris's (Trinidad) 'Child this is the gospel on bakes'
  c. Cynthia James's (Trinidad) 'the anatomy of race'
  d. Olive Senior's (Jamaica) 'Nansi 'Tory'
- Edwidge Dandicat, 'Children of the Sea' from *Krik? Krak!* (1991)

Course Description:
A survey course of literature by women from Africa, the Caribbean, and North America, it seeks to introduce the writers, their works and the experiences that inform their writings. Beginning with a consideration of traditional African oral forms, through the initial experiences in the New World, to more modern representations of literature, the course foregrounds African and Diasporan experiences of women. Some of these may be sociological, political, and/or economic factors. It will examine the diverse ways deployed by women to discuss issues that are relevant to them as well as the techniques and recurring motifs used in their works. Among the authors read are Buchi Emecheta from Nigeria, Mariama Ba from Senegal, and Alice Walker from the United States and in addition, excerpts from the work of Patricia Hill Collins, Obioma Nnaemeka, Edwidge Dandicat, Jamaica Kincaid, Maryse Conde, bell hooks, Toni Cade Bambara, and more. Some of the issues explored are feminism, womanism, sexism, patriarchy, racism and classism as well as maternity and independence, mammies, matriarchs, and other controlling images of black women.

Course Objectives:
Students will be able to:
- Demonstrate in writing an awareness of the depth and scope of the contributions of women of African descent throughout the world to an international literary canon.

- Define and enumerate who many of the contemporary African women writers of the diaspora are.
- Compare and contrast feminism and womanism and list the six distinguishing features of Black Feminist Thought.
- Analyze and explain the connections between a writer's life/culture and her work.
- Show from the historical perspective the development of the various literary genres that women writers of the African world have espoused.
- Examine the themes and issues that face African and Diasporan women that are depicted in the required novels read.
- Compare and contrast the portrayal of male and female characters in the novels of Emecheta, Ba, and Walker.
- Compile the authors' literary techniques and special stylistic features used in their novels.
- Appraise the novels' value to the contemporary English-speaking world literary canon.
- Summarize the impact that these female authors had on you as a person.

Grades:

Discussion Board participation	10 X 30 points)	300 points
Quizzes	(3 X 50 points)	150 points
2 Short Papers	(2 X 125 points)	250 points
Final Project – 4th Novel/Author of Choice Study		300 points
	TOTAL	**1,000 points**
(See examples of possible ways to earn at end of syllabus)	Extra Credit	100 points

COURSE POLICIES
Attendance and Commitment
- Read the assignments for each week; submit work on **Sunday** by midnight.
- Participate, participate, participate – the Discussion Board is what makes this course more than a correspondence course.
- Treat everyone's work and ideas with **respect,** including your own.

Revisions:
Any assignment on which you get less than a 'C' or less should be rewritten after a conference with me. If you are dissatisfied with your grade, you may also rewrite assignments after a conference with me. Revisions are <u>due one week </u>after the assignment is returned. For final grading, I average the two grades.

Plagiarism/Academic Dishonesty:
All assignments should be your own original work, not material copied from other classrooms, the internet, or textbooks and commercial materials. If you draw from other sources, you should cite them using MLA format Assignments should be written for this class alone.

TENTATIVE SYLLABUS
I reserve the right to make changes in this syllabus if necessary fro the benefit of the class and will provide you with a revised syllabus if this occurs. Input can be made from the class during the first week.

NOTE: <u>Assignments</u> are due on **Sundays** by **midnight.**
<u>Discussion Board:</u> First posting due by **Thursday;** final posting by **Sunday** midnight.

Week 1	<u>INTRODUCTION</u>
1/06	This first week is meant to get us better acquainted with each
Wed	other and Africa before beginning our academic tasks.
	Lecture: Africa is not a Country
	Assignment: Introduce yourselves through the Discussion Board. Fill out the Information
	Sheet under the Assignments Tab. View Power Point 'The African Continent'
	Check your knowledge of African countries by playing a game – see link.
	NOTE: Everything is due at the end of the Week (Sunday at midnight).
Week 2	<u>FEMINISM – Defining and Relating to Women's Issues</u>
1/11	**Discussion #1** (30 pts) 'Has the Feminist movement made
Mon	life in the U.S. better?
	Assignment: Read Betty Friedan's <u>Chapter 1</u>, *The Feminist Mystique.* Check under the Documents Tab for the link to this text and three other links on Friedan & Feminism
Week 3	<u>FEMINISM AND AFRICAN WOMANISM: CONTRADIC-TORY OR COMPLEMENTARY?</u>
1/19	**Discussion #2** (30 pts) Check for topic under Discussion
Tue	Board Tab.
	Assignment: Read 3 articles: 'Feminism & African Woman-hood,' by 'Zulu Sofola; 'Women & Creative Writing in Africa,' by Flora Nwapa; 'North American Feminisms/Global Feminisms – Contradiction or Complementary?' by Angel Miles. See Documents Tab
Week 4	*<u>The Joys of Motherhood,</u> –* <u>INTRODUCTION TO AUTHOR AND CULTURE</u>
1/25	**Discussion #3** (30 pts) Topic under Discussion Board Tab

Mon	**Assignment:** Read Chapters 1-5 of *JM* (*The Joys of Motherhood*) pp 7-62
Week 5	*The Joys of Motherhood* THE WOMAN AS A WRITER IN CONTEMPORARY AFRICA
2/01	**Discussion #4** (30 pts) Topic under Discussion Board Tab
Mon	**Assignment:** Read Chapters 6-9 of *JM* pp 63-110
Week 6	*The Joys of Motherhood* THE AFRICAN LITERARY RENAISSANCE
2/8	**Discussion #5** (30 pts) Topic under Discussion Board Tab
Mon	**Assignment:** Read Chapters 10-14 of *JM* pp 111-169
Week 7	*The Joys of Motherhood* LANGUAGE, IMAGERY, AND THEME
2/15	**Discussion None** as you prepare for your first quiz & finish reading
Mon	**Assignment:** Finish reading *JM*
	Quiz #1 (50 pts) over *The Joys of Motherhood* **Due Sunday** 2/21
Week 8	ISLAMIC CULTURE & FEMINISM (*Woman at Point Zero* OR *So Long a Letter*)
2/22	**Discussion #6** (30 pts) Topic under Discussion Board Tab
Mon	**Assignment:** Read *WPZ* Chap. 1 & 2 (pp 1-42); OR *SLL* Chap 1-10 (pp 1-25)
	PAPER 1 (125 pts) DUE on **Sunday** 2/28
WINTER BREAK (HOLIDAY) MARCH 1-7	
Week 9	NAWAL EL SAADAWI & MARIAMA BA (*Woman at Point Zero/So Long a Letter*)
3/8	**Discussion #7** (30 pts) Topic under Discussion Board Tab
Mon	**Assignment:** Read *WPZ* Chap 2 (pp 42-72); OR *SLL* Chap 11-17 (pp 26-56)
Week 10	WOMEN'S ISSUES IN AFRICA (*Woman or Point Zero/So Long a Letter*)
3/15	**Discussion #8** (30 pts) Topic under Discussion Board Tab
Mon	**Assignment:** Finish reading *WPZ* OR *SLL*
	Quiz #2 (50 pts) on *Woman at Point Zero* OR *So Long a Letter* **Due Sunday** 3/21
Week 11	DIASPORAN WOMEN WRITERS (THE CARIBBEAN)
3/22	**Discussion** Sharing of poetry – post a favorite and explain
Mon	why it is
	Assignment: Read selected poems and short stories posted under Documents
	PAPER 2 (125 pts) DUE on **Sunday** 3/28
Week 12	BLACK FEMINIST THOUGHT *The Color Purple,* Alice Walker
3/29	**Discussion #9** (30 pts) Topic under Discussion Board Tab
Mon	**Assignment:** Read *CP* pp. 1-106 (Letters 1-44)

Read Chap 1 & 2 *Black Feminist Thought,* Patricia Hill Collins under Documents

Week 13   AFRICAN AMERICAN FEMALE WRITERS *The Color Purple*
4/5   **Discussion #10** (30 pts) Topic under Discussion Board Tab
Mon   **Assignment:** Read *CP* pp. 107-191 (Letters 45-72)

Week 14   AFRICAN AMERICAN FEMALE WRITERS *The Color Purple*
4/12   **Discussion #11** (Bonus 30 pts)
Mon   **Assignment:** Finish *CP* pp. 192-288 (Letters 72-90)
      Quiz #3 (50 pts) over *The Color Purple*   **Due Sunday 4/18**

Week 15   **Final Project • Due Thursday 4/22**
4/19

EXTRA CREDIT OPTIONS (50 points each)
NOTE: Each option listed below is a suggestion of what you could do to earn extra credit. If you have an idea of something you would like to do that is not on this list, please bring it to my attention so that we may consider it.

[1.] **Movie Review**   Below are a few of the films I think you would find interesting and relevant in the classroom. Some are available from the Department of Africana Studies* while others would need to be rented from a video store. The Flint Public Library has a great collection of documentary films.

The Boys of Baraka	12 twelve-year-old boys from Baltimore are sent to school in Kenya for a year. How this affects their lives is remarkable.
*Africa: Episodes 1-8 * *	A National Geographic series that presents Africa through the eyes of its people, conveying the diversity and beauty of the land and the compelling personal stories of the people who shape its future.
The Invisible Children	3 young, white, American men film the children in northern Uganda who are targets of the Lord's Resistance Army.
Moulade	Directed by the Senegalese writer and film maker Ousmane Sembene – his last film – a powerful story about female circumcision (4 girls run away from their initiation rites circle and get protection from a woman in their village).
Blood Diamonds	Sierra Leone is torn apart by the diamond trade
Catch a Fire	set in apartheid South Africa
Sierra Leone Refugee All Stars *	A reggae-inflected band born in the camps of West Africa, represents a real life story of survival and hope. The six member Refugee All Stars came

together in Guinea after civil war forced them from their native Sierra Leone. Traumatized by physical injuries and the brutal loss of family and community, they fight back with the only means they have – music**. Part of the POV movie series on campus** 3/17

Rubric: A one-two page review which would include a brief summary of the film and a suggestion on how it could b e useful or not so useful in your classroom. Or a movie poster or brochure could serve to summarize the film.

[2.] **Book Review** The authors that we read for this course have written other books which may be of interest. A few of these are listed below. Additional authors whose works you might find enjoyable are also listed. See me if you have any particular book in mind or if you want to know of other works in poetry or drama as well.

- **Nawal El Saadawi,** *A Daughter of Isis* the first volume of her auto-biography
- **Chinua Achebe**, *No Longer at Ease* or *Anthills of the Savanna*
- **Ngugi wa Thiong'o,** *Weep Not Child*   set in Kenya – a story with the Mau Mau resistance to the British as back drop
- **J. Nozipo Maraire,** *Zenzele* set in Zimbabwe, a Zimbabwean mother sharing her wisdom with her America-bound daughter through a series of thoughtful letters.

RUBRIC: The book report can be a standard one-two page review which summarizes the story with some analysis of the plot, setting, characters, theme, etc., OR it could be creative and done to fit your talents/skills – an interesting book cover and blurb for the back cover, a musical rendition of a theme or main character, etc.

[3.] **Poetry Collection** Selection of favorite poems from West, East, and/or Southern Africa either by the same author or different authors either by author or by theme/topic. If you had 20 poems, you could do a poem a day for a month. A minimum of 10 would be required. Introduce the collection in 2-3 paragraphs.

RUBRIC: Points would be awarded according to the number collected and a brief introduction to the collection:
10 poems for 18 points
15 poems for 20 points
20 poems for 25 points

[4.] **Recipe Collection/Visit to an African Restaurant** Selection of favorite recipes from a region or country in Africa. At least two of the recipes must be cooked and tasted with reviews of the results by those tasting (family, friends, fellow students!)

OR

Eat at an African restaurant – I know of the Blue Nile in Ann Arbor, for example – and submit the menu along with what you ordered and what you learned about the dishes, how the food was served, and what ingredients were used.

RUBRIC: Points would be awarded according to the authenticity of the recipes and how they reflect the uniqueness of the region or country they are from either in ingredients used or style/method of cooking and preparation. Substitutions for certain unattainable ingredients would be accepted if necessary.

[5.] **Interview with an African** Interview an African about his/her country. Prepare about 15 questions in advance and add any that come to mind during the interview. Select someone from a country you want to learn more about or someone who can discus certain topics (the role of women in modern Nigerian society) of interest to you. If you want to discuss possible people, I can suggest a few friends (Nigeria, Eritrea, Ethiopia, Uganda, Cameroon, for a start)

RUBRIC: The tape of the interview or a written reproduction of the interview documenting the person interviewed, questions asked & answered, the date, time, and location of the interview. Any observations about how the interview went. Did the person speak freely on all issues?

Helen Chukwuma

Introduction

One of the challenges of teaching African literature in the academy is culture disparity. From the outset difference can often be construed as inferiority. Western students' previous exposure to the continent and its affairs is generally limited and at best negative. This calls for a patient reorientation of students to the new realities that are African. Students have first to learn that the geographical entity called Africa is not a country but a continent and the second largest continent, second only to Asia in the world. The continent because of its vastness is divided into regions: north Africa, west, east, central and south Africa. The geographical considerations also include cultures, peoples and religion. The history of the continent also forms part of the introduction. This includes slavery, colonialism, post-colonialism, urbanization, neo-colonialism and imperialism. The new movement of globalization which throws borders open, forces a knowledge and appreciation of cultures and peoples, languages and literatures.

Culture is a way of life, the way a people organize their lives around certain norms, values , belief systems and religious practices. A people's culture is basically what works for them and no one culture is superior or inferior to another. Students have to be led towards an appreciation of this fact and to understand and respect other people's values, differences and diversity. In the West the general information on Africa in the news media is dark, exotic, mysterious and deadly.

The Tarzan myths about primitiveness and barbarism have to be reconstructed to make room for modern day realities which research, trade and globalization have made possible. Africa's history written by Africans themselves is available and this helps to set the records straight.

The same can be said of the literature – Joseph Conrad's novel with its telling title *Heart of Darkness* and Joyce Cary's *Mister Johnson* being cases in point. It was their warped portraiture of African characters, society and environment that propelled Chinua Achebe to write *Things Fall Apart* in subtle refutation. Man's basic humanity and the commonality of human emotions and experiences remain basic to life on our planet. Great literature captures this and renders it relevant for all time.

World Literature and African Literature

With multiculturalism is joined *Weltliteratur* (World Literature, a term coined by Johan Wolfgang von Goethe during a conversation with his disciple and protegé Johan Peter Eckerman in 1827), Comparative Literature and Translation. This idea as mooted by Goethe, took wing and developed as a full discipline in the academy at the turn of the century. In 2006, David Damrosch in the introduction to his text *The Idea of World Literature: History and Pedagogical Practices*, asks 'Which Literature? and 'Whose World?' How do we cross boundaries of culture without offending or condescending? What is the place of African literature in this compendium of world literature? The twentieth century witnessed the rise of world markets, the movement of peoples and goods, great technological advancement in transportation and communication links, and space technology, to the extent that the world has shrunk and is now considered a global village. It is to Goethe's credit that he foresaw the same trends in literary production and consumption which would transcend national boundaries to assume a global form. He saw the crossing of national boundaries of literature as a healthy fertilization of ideas that engenders growth and freshness. Based on his experience with Chinese and French literature, he welcomed the unique perspectives of readers of a foreign language and culture to his works. World literature to him was a coming together of varied interpretations and appreciation of works of art beyond the output of the writer and the confines of his culture and nation.

I define World literature therefore as a dalliance of inclusiveness portraying literature as a universal possession of mankind. World literature literally means world culture because through literature, culture is exposed and transmitted. World literature celebrates difference with an underlay which forms the foundation of a splendid mosaic which is not at all homogenous but whose ingenious artistry throws up the beauty of the human mind and creative spirit. It depicts how cultures utilize their creativity to add to the beauty of the universe in sights, sounds and imagination. This dovetails to the following discussion of accessibility of African literature and the problem of indigenous languages in its writing.

The Language of African Literature

Language is the core of cultural identity. It carries the burden of a people's name. Thus the Igbo speak Igbo, the Hausa speak Hausa and the English

speak English. But what do Nigerians speak?' Nigerian? What do Cameroonians speak? And the same question can be asked of most African
nations without a viable answer. This indeed is the sad condition of the
linguistic quagmire of post-colonized nations. This was the concern of Obi
Wali in 1962, and the concern of Ngugi wa Thiongo. The language problem
remains an albatross in creative writing in the continent. Ngugi's view is
in consonance with Obi Wali's and he used Gikuyu in all his creative
works starting with *Devil on the Cross* (1980) first published in Gikuyu as
Caitaani Mutharaba-ini (1979). Ngugi relies on translation for his works
to be read outside his homeland Kenya. He sometimes does the translation himself. This of course is like repeating the creative process. This is
Ngugi's way of sloughing off the linguistic colonialism involved in using
the colonialist's language. This is as commendable, but carries its own
constraints and challenges. These range from grammar of usage, to production costs and readership. Most of us read Ngugi in translation but
note and welcome his stand.

Chinua Achebe, on the other hand, offers neither apology nor remorse
for writing in the English language. He took the tool of the master, made it
his own and forced it to yield to the particular nuances that communicate
his own reality and experience (1975:55-62). This way, he has assured a
readership that crosses most national boundaries.

Both positions serve the users' purposes. English as a language is so
ultra-metropolitan that the academy talks of 'Englishes' not just English,
thereby showing the world-wide plurality of its usage; to the extent that in
Linguistics, British English is used to designate the English spoken in
England and American English, that spoken in the United States. Nigeria
has over three hundred and fifty languages and English is the second and
official language. Most of post-colonial Africa reflects the same linguistic
predicament, also found in Francophone and Lusophone countries. All
told, Achebe's position remains the viable option in the political reality of
the time. Ngugi's position is idealistic and futuristic and most writers
have not taken it up.

Language remains the last frontier in decolonization. The process of
language evolution takes centuries and some countries such as Nigeria
have adopted a language policy that will eventually define and stamp
their autonomy. The implication of language and African literature is that
most of what is available especially in oral literature is in translation.

There is an ardent need also to preserve writings in their languages of
origin, this way they will be available to scholars who may wish to study
these works in their original language; for indeed, translations are at best
'remains' of the original. The very obvious advantage of translation is that
the literature is accessible and enjoys world-wide readership. This brings
in its wake, recognition, exposure, popularity and economic boost. African
writers such as Wole Soyinka, Chinua Achebe, Ama Ata Aidoo, Nadine
Gordimer, Doris Lessing, Helon Habila, Chimamanda Adichie, Sefi Atta,

Uwem Akpan and others have received world honours from the Nobel Prize, to the Noma award, and the Man Booker and Commonweath prizes.

Delineations of African Literature

1. Geography:
Africa as a continent has suffered from truncations of its land mass. The division of the world into the technologically advanced as well as the age-old canker worm of race has forced a situation whereby Egypt and North African countries have been excised and dangle between the Mediter-ranean Sea and the Sahara desert. The misnomer of labelling the current revolutions (2011) in Algeria, Tunisia and Egypt as that of the Middle East is a gross undermining of the continent's political integrity. Lately, informed judgement has prevailed and those countries have been returned to their motherland. The term Sub-Saharan Africa carries with it an implied divisive judgement. Africa stands by geographical boundaries of accepted usage as North, South, East, West and Central Africa. These labels communicate effectively the nations in question and new informa-tion technology with its attendant gadgets enables students and researchers to quickly access and locate countries on the global map, thereby removing all ambiguity of placement.

2. Historiography and Colonialism:
Teaching African literature demands situating the writers in their histori-cal backgrounds. This is of paramount importance for the understanding of literacy and the commitment of the African writer. Oral literature remains as culture-bound as it has always been. With colonialism and the advent of western literacy, writing flowered. Some early African writers looked inwards to tell their story e.g, T. Mofolo wrote on the Zulu warrior Chaka. The history of the nefarious trans-Atlantic slavery is the backdrop for appreciating the slave narrative of Olaudah Equiano, Gustavus Vassa, the African. Most early African literature in poetry and fiction drew strength and subject matter from the process of colonization and the fight for independence. Thus literature trends and issues remain bound to the state of the nations. As I argued elsewhere (2003), 'There is much to be said about the views of the insider pressing home an awakening of self.'

The subject matter of the African novel therefore is realistic and socially conditioned. In this regard, African literature should be seen in its histori-cal context in terms of the reality that has shaped and continues to shape the consciousness of the writers and their responses in the novels they write. 'This reality is not static but changes all the time' (vi). While the Anglophone writers wrote about their home culture and life before the advent of the white man as a way of reclaiming their identity, (see novels of cultural nationalism such as Achebe's *Things Fall Apart, Arrow of God;*

Ayi Kwei Armah's *Two Thousand Seasons*; Camara Laye's *The African Child*; Ngugi wa Thiongo's *Weep Not Child* and others) Francophone writers were combating the assimilation policy of the French colonialists by introducing the political and cultural movement of Negritude in the thirties.

Thus the teaching of African literature in 'modern times' needs to be grounded in the literary theories of Negritude, New Historicism and Culturalism. The critical theory of New Historicism posits that a literary work is not created in a vacuum and does not just reflect the work of a single mind but is impacted by events in time and place where the author lived and worked. This underscores the importance of history and literary history.

Other issues that impact African literature are urbanization, wars, political disillusionment, gender, military governance, natural disasters, pandemics, persecutions, civil strife and social issues, such as human trafficking and others (see Charles Nnolim, *Approaches to the African Novel*, 1992). These issues have historical documentation and their study is viewed from the impact they have on the people's lives.

3. 'Temptation of "Imposition of Domestic Literary Values" on a foreign work':

This is one of Damrosch's concerns which I share. Language is the vehicle of literature as well as the core of culture as in it are encased the people's values, norms and belief systems. With the variability that attends world literature, the tendency is for a foreign reader of African literature to impose his own literary values. Goethe would not have seen this as problem, because he believed and accepted German literary taste as dominant. This however cannot be said for literature of other countries outside the western world. How do teachers and students respond to cultural differences or projecting their own values into the analysis and interpretation of texts? How do students approach the new, the quaint and the novel? Teachers should adopt an analytical approach that shows novelty as an artificial coating which if stripped away the reader arrives at the core of the narrative which throws up the commonality of the human experience so that it is not novel at all. For example, the tragedy of Okonkwo in *Things Fall Apart* shows up similarities of the human excesses and flaws in a tragic character recognizable in other tragic characters such as Macbeth or Hamlet. Cultural differences add embellishments to literature and African literature should be appreciated in that regard. African literature exposes the inner rhythms of the continent and situates it in a multicultural world.

Our critics have established the aesthetics and criticism of African literature. I refer specifically to the critical works of Chinua Achebe, *Morning Yet on Creation Day* (1975), *Hopes and Impediments* (1988); Wole Soyinka, *Myth, Literature and the African World* (1975), *Drama and the African World View*; Abiola Irele, *The Negritude Movement* (2010),

The African Imagination: Literature in Africa and the Black Diaspora (2001), *The African Experience in Literature and Ideology* (1981).

Anthologies and Expositions

The fact that African literature is thriving today is due primarily to its expositions in anthologies and certain publishing houses and journals. Special tribute must be paid to Alan Hill, the Englishman who founded the African Writers Series and Heinemann Educational Books in 1960. From 1962 to early 2000, it provided a vast reliable platform for the publication and exposure of the vibrant literature from the continent. An associate in the enterprise, Keith Sambrook joined the team as its marketer. James Currey informs us that it was the team of Aigboje Higo and Chinua Achebe who attracted and captured many of the outstanding writers from West Africa, making writing from that region phenomenal. The East African branch of the series owes its function to the sagacity of Henry Chakava of Kenya in the early years of that nation's independence. The Heinemann African Writers Series was the enabling factor in the spread and dissemination of African literature.

Chinua Achebe played a pivotal role in encouraging young writers from the continent. Ngugi attests to this (Currey, 23) for it was Achebe who recommended Ngugi's first novel *Weep Not Child* to the Heinemann publishers. The African Literature Association of the United States of America has our gratitude and acclaim for the great relevance and visibility it gave and continues to give to African literature by providing the platform and forum for scholastic exchange in conferences and publications. A new phase of publishing in African literature has come with the emergence of Africa World Press and its vibrant projection of literary works from the continent.

Later, journals continued this exposure in critical essays and analysis of this literature. Bernth Lindfors and his work as editor of *Research in African Literatures* for decades, Eldred Durosimi Jones who handed over the editorship of *African Literature Today* to Ernest Emenyonu in 2000 deserve a mention as do the late Sunday Anozie and his journal *The Conch*. A polemical move to expose young minds to the opportunity of publishing was made by the master himself, Chinua Achebe, when he established the *Okike* journal in the University of Nigeria, Nsukka, in 1971. Other journals such as *Présence Africaine*, published in France, also helped develop African literature.

Mitigating Factors in Teaching African Literature

First in this list is publication access. There are many literary works being produced in the continent but there are very limited facilities for publication and marketing abroad. Further, printing costs are high. Africans of means need to invest in their literature in order to enable it to be accessible. James Currey and the African Writers Series have played a role, but in the age of globalization and multiculturalism, African voices must continue to be heard, must continue to count. The problem can be diagnosed as economic but even this emanates to a large extent from the misgovernance and corruption of our leaders. This needs urgent redress.

The second factor is attendant on the first and that is the non-availability of the books once they have been produced. The movement and sale of books from the continent to the outside world have not been streamlined. Many books are trapped in warehouses, not reaching potential readers. This happens across continents. I say this from my experience of teaching African literature on both sides of the Atlantic. Workshops are needed to address this artificial dearth of literary works from Africa.

The third factor is the need to facilitate faculty and student visits to regions of Africa. This could take the form of summer programs where both teachers and students experience at first hand the land and people they read about. It can be highly exciting and revealing.

Conclusion

Literacy in the present age is becoming more complex with the speedy demands of information technology. Globalization and multiculturalism have broken down barriers of solitude and isolation. African literature is a canon which having emerged from the difficulties of the past, urgently needs to continue the momentum by rendering our literature more visible and accessible.

WORKS CITED

Achebe, Chinua. *Morning Yet on Creation Day*. London: Heinemann Educational Books, 1975.

—— *Hopes and Impediments*. London: Heinemann, 1988.

Chukwuma, Helen. *Accents in the African Novel*. Port Harcourt, Nigeria: Pearl Publishers. 2nd ed., 2003.

—— *Igbo Oral Literature, Theory and Tradition*. Pearl Publishers, 2nd ed., 2002.

Currey, James. *Africa Writes Back*. Oxford: James Currey Publishers, 2008.

Damrosch, David. *What is World Literature?* Princeton University Press, 2003

Kalu, Anthonia C. ed. *The Rienner Anthology of African Literature*. Lynne Rienner Publishers Inc., 2007.

Meli, Francis *et al*. 'The Role of Culture in the African Revolution: Ngugi wa Thiong'o and Mongane Wally Serote in a round table discussion', *Ngugi wa Thiong'o Speaks, Interviews with the Kenyan Writer*. Eds Reinhard Sander & Bernth Lindfors. Trenton, New Jersey: Africa World Press Inc., 2006.

Mezu, Rose Ure. *Chinua Achebe, The Man and his Works. London*: Adonis & Abbey, 2006.

Mikics, David. *A New Handbook of Literary Terms.* Yale University Press, 2007.

Nnolim, Charles. *Approaches to the African Novel.* Port Harcourt, Nigeria: Saros International Publication, 1992.

Owomoyela. Onyekan. *The Columbia Guide to West African Literature in English Since 1945.* New York: Columbia University Press, 2008.

Challenges & Prospects
of Teaching Oral Literature in Africa:
A Teacher's Perspective

Mark Ighile

The question of the continuation of the teaching of oral literature in Africa has generated considerable tension among teachers and researchers. While some fear that the discipline is doomed, others tend to take solace in the age-old saying that culture never dies. Uncertainty about the survival of the African's cultural heritage continues and this article examines the future of teaching and of research in oral literature in Africa against a backdrop of misconceptions and the evolution of globalization which takes its toll on the indigenous lifestyle. The discourse will begin with a brief history of the collection of oral materials, the roots of oral literary teaching and research, and the present state and future of oral literary scholarship. This triangular approach is similar to that of one of the oldest African teachers of oral literature, Taban Lo Liyong, with his 1972 indices for the sustainability of the verbal art. In his opinion, for verbal art to thrive, teachers and scholars must act as the legendary strange beast with three heads. One head must look perpetually behind to capture the past; one must look steadily under the feet to grasp the present realities while the third head must stay focused on the future for a clearer vision (ix).

Another early teacher of oral literature in Africa, Isidore Okpewho (1992), has stressed the inadequacies of previous studies of African oral literature especially those by foreign scholars due to their wrong attitudes. Most of these early scholars believed that Africans were 'primitive' and 'savage' and therefore had no capacity for sophisticated and imaginative forms of expression. They had no respect for the things Africans said and the way they said them. They therefore, represented their forms in a rather reckless manner and consequently shortchanged indigenous African culture. However, when indigenous African scholars eventually emerged, the attitude towards oral literary research changed for the positive.

A Brief Historical Survey

It is instructive at this juncture to briefly trace the history of the study of

African oral literature, with a view to not only attempting to correct the various misconceptions about Africa and oral literature, but also to assess with historical sensibility, the sources for the study and teaching of African oral literature. In doing this, our approach would be to articulate the three cardinal interests: The first, 'in culture' popularly nourished by the evolutionists, the second 'in society' an approach associated with British anthropologists, Bronislaw Malinowski and A.R. Radcliffe-Brown, and the American Franz Boas. The third point of interest which is 'in literature' carries a weight that is indeed enormous. As well as revolutionising the study and teaching of African oral literature, this interest has helped in projecting the beauty of African literary ideals. Babalola's *The Content and Form of Yoruba Ijala* (1966), Kunene's *A Heroic Poetic of the Basotho (1971)* and Kofi Awoonor's *Guardian of the Sacred Word* (1974) to cite a few instances, aptly illustrate the varieties of the literary off shoot.

Early citings of African oral literature (folklore) can be traced back to European travellers who wrote descriptions of the culture and essence of the African kingdoms they encountered in their wanderings in 1550. However, the European travellers at that time illuminated aspects of the African oral literature but were not really concerned with the overall realization of oral literature. The earliest collection of verbal arts, south of the Sahara, is the 231 aphorism published by J. Dard in 1826 (meantioned in Bascom, 1964). This was followed by 43 Wolof fables collected by Roger, a Frenchman in 1828.

The first tangible monograph on Nigerian folktales appeared in London in 1854 when Rev. S. Koelle, a German missionary and linguist, published his *African Native Literature of Proverbs, Tales, Fables and Historical Fragments in the Kanuri or Borno language*. A number of collections of African oral literature appeared in German, an example of which is Wilhelm Bleak's *Reineke Pucns* 1896 and other publications of 1887 and 1896. In 1877, a collection of Malagasy narratives was published by Norwegian missionary, Lars Dahle and in 1899, Gabriel Ferand, after some research, published a collection of tales, *Contes Populairs Malasqachies* (Paris, Ernest Leroux 1893). In South Africa in 1882 George McCall Theal published a collection of 21 tales translated into English by a Xhoe speaker.

Observations abound as to the workings of the historical movement. The first is that the early documents provided a credible foundation for refutation, as Finnegan (1970) also puts it, of 'the popular European image of Africa as totally without literary pretensions' (27). The second point is the emergence of linguistic studies as a specialist and scholarly field. This had an immediate effect on oral scholarship and began collection of African texts and translations. African literary study was at this time dominated by missionaries and colonial civil servants but the influence and the activities of the anthropologist in the first half of the twentieth century cannot be overstressed.

From 1910, scholars like Leo Frobenius began to draw attention to the existence of African oral narratives and other arts in his *Atlantishe Goetterlarbe*. Carl Meinhof's work of narrative comparison in 1911 was also of immense relevance in this context. While in Malagasy, Charles Renel was getting through with the publication of his volumes in 1910 of Ikantea *de Madagascar*, John Moscoe was in a different setting publishing *The Ragarda: An Account of their Native Customs and Myths* in 1911. In 1912, Amaury Talbot published *In the Shadow of the Bush*.

It may be important to add here the prominence of Hausa folklore over other language lores. For within a very short time, three Hausa publications came to the limelight. The folk literatures were *Tatsuniyoyi Na Hausa (*1911*) Hausa Folklores* (1913) and *Hausa Superstition and Custom* (1913) It was not until 1929 that the first Nigerian M.J. Ogunmefu came out with his 'Yoruba legend'. Thereafter, many Nigerians joined the train with remarkable contributions. From 1948-52, E. N. Amaku published five volumes of Efik Folktales entitled 'Edikot Nwed Mbuk' in Efik. Others such as Yoruba novelists Daniel Fagunwa and Amos Tutuola had, by 1952, started making use of folklore in their writings.

From the late 1950s and 1960s, things took a new shape and the field of oral literary research began to gain impetus. Many Africans had begun to take an interest in the collection of folktales. S.M. Mofokeng's 'The Development of the Leading Figures in Animal Tales in Africa' (1955), Babalola's 'Yoruba Folktales' (*West Africa Review* 1962, 48-9) and much later Clark's performance of the Ozidi Saga were reflections of this literary outburst. Moreover, there was a rapidly growing interest in African Studies as a whole, manifested in the recognition of Africa as a worthwhile field of academic study and a radical offshoot of professional scholars concerned with various parts of African life. Work, therefore, became increasingly specialized.

The general environment of the time encouraged the recognition of scholarly work and this in effect broadened the interests of certain professional students of Africa. Earlier forsaken fields were embraced again. The consequence of all these phenomena, as Ruth Finnegan (1970) also observes is 'some renewal of interest in African oral literary study' (41). Apart from questioning earlier thought and positions on pre-colonial African stories and folktales, some of these tales had revealed themselves to be of historical, mythological, legendary and epical significance. This period also illuminated the domination of the oral literary environment by anthropologist. The emergence of African oral literary study as a major new field of ethnographic research is evident in the growing number of books of scholarly interest published. Dorson's *African Folklore,* 1972, and Bernth Lindfors' edited *Forms of Folklore* 1977 are ready examples. Fieldwork on African epics such as the translated

Sunjata: An Epic of Old Mali 1965 and Okpewho's *The Epic in Africa* 1979 readily served as immediate tools of illustration.

Following the Chadwicks' and Ruth Finnegan's claims of an absence of epic tradition in Africa, Isidore Okpewho in his 'Does Epic exist in Africa?' (1988) and John William Johnson 'Yes Virginia, There is an Epic in Africa' (1980) set out to refute the misconception. The publication of *Epic in Africa* by Okpewho is an attempt by the author to provide a strong direction for oral literary study through a profound general investigation. Okpewho while addressing what he calls 'the tyranny of ethnographic data' (1980, 443) wonders what the difference really is between epic and heroic tales. Some Africans had taken up studies of their own folk narratives in the 1950s and mid-1960s e.g. Mofokeng (1955), Babalola 1952 and Ikiddeh 1966.

Today in Perspective

Since the second half of the twentieth cantury, scholars have been teaching and writing significantly on African oral literature and for that long, the subject had been in the syllabus of some African universities. Perhaps it should be placed on record the fact that the substantial work of W.H. Whiteley, *A Selection of African Prose 1: Traditional Oral Texts* came out in 1964 leading some twenty titles in the next ten years in the Oxford Library of African Literature. It was that series that produced Finnegan's epoch-making work, *Oral Literature in Africa* in 1970. Daniel Kunene's *Heroic Poetry of the Basotho* published in 1971, and described by Abdulkadir (1981) as an aspect of 'African oral song which tries to eliminate certain misconceptions of heroic poetry in Africa' (33), was also influential.

Since oral literature was not part of the academic tradition of the West, it had little chance, as Ikiddeh (1987) also argues, in the first place, of being on the educational curriculum of colonial institutions. However, after the educational policy-making process had passed into the hands of the natives, things took a different shape. And they have continued to improve ever since. Oral literature is now taught in many African universities and as observed by Okanlawon (1983), it is 'fast becoming one of the most popular disciplines in the humanities' (74). While it is to Isidore Okpewho's credit that the study of oral literature as a literary discipline was established in the Department of English, University of Ibadan, Nigeria, it is to Taban Lo Liyong's credit and that of a few others that oral literary study became popular at the University of Nairobi, Kenya, to cite just two instances.

My Teaching and Research Experience

It should be noted that the status of oral literature, as a course of study in higher institutions, still needs to be enhanced. While some African scholars have established its relevance and equality, in relation to other subjects in the humanities, others have continued to wonder whether it should be fully integrated into the mainstream literary department. But perhaps crucial to the promotion of oral literary teaching and research in Africa, is the need to stress the importance of fieldwork. This emphasis will not only keep oral literature alive, but it will also reawaken the consciousness of our young scholars and students to the foundation of their traditional heritage. Quite an appreciable number of students believe that oral literature can be taught, and research carried out, without necessarily having recourse to the oral artists in their locality. While some claim that they have never had any interaction with a performer or artist, others have expressed fear about the dire religious implication of such cultural contacts. A '300 level' undergraduate student of Oral literature at Redeemer's University in Nigeria did not hide her feelings, in one of our lecture series:

> Sir, I cannot see myself going to the village to conduct interview with a medicine man or a masquerade in the name of carrying out research. What if he decides to initiate me into his diabolical cult? Or how do I attend and cover a traditional funeral ceremony without really knowing the unwritten rules guiding such cultural events? I trust my parents. They will not even allow me go into such delicate adventure.

Over the years, however, we have tried to locate the fulfilment of oral literary scholarship in the healthy relationship between the researcher (in this case, the students, and at some points, the lecturer and the students) and the oral artists. Several lecture periods have been converted to meeting sessions with some traditional poets, musicians and performers. The outcome has been quite rewarding. This, in a way, explains why Wambara (2005) advocates a participatory research in oral literature in which the researcher, the audience, and the artists actually discuss and learn from each other. It is a situation where all actors grow as the performance process unfolds and progresses. A truly participatory oral literature research activity is enriched with indigenous knowledge and strives to empower the source community to reflect on their performances in order to improve on them. Recalling some of the research visits he has conducted in rural and urban communities, Wambara notes that the decline in the popularity of oral literature in contemporary society is occasioned by the ever-widening gaps between the oral artists, the audience and the teacher/researcher. In other words, while the oral artist is deemed to be quaint, traditional and therefore, irrelevant, the audience is perceived to be mean, sophisticated and too demanding, and the teacher/researcher is dismissed as a detached and verbose stranger. It should be observed that this situation creates a dispirited nature of the art. In this context, a teacher/researcher is expected to build bridges of understanding to ensure harmony between the artist, the scholar and the audience. triangle in oral literature composition, performance and scholarship, which in turn, dilutes the transactional.

Anene-Boyle (2002), who has conducted several research works on the Niger-Delta artists of Nigeria, shares more-or-less the same position. He believes that for oral literary scholarship to make sense and have a future, the age-long distrust between the artist and the researcher must be removed. His fear is that:

> Artists do not regard the researcher as part of them. In spite of trying to put them at ease by giving financial incentives among other strategies, they do not treat the researcher as a native. The result is that because of the communication gap, they would not be inclined to trust the stranger with intimate aspects of their tradition. (44).

Besides, there is the need for the scholar/researcher to get closer to home and integrate with his people. As Anene-Boyle also observes, there are several advantages of carrying out research work in a place as near as possible to one's culture. To begin with, the feeling of intimacy and welcome can be very overwhelming and encouraging. There is also the joy of realizing that one is helping to keep the cherished tradition of one's own people alive. One is also bound to have great respect rather than contempt when appreciating the level of skill and sophistication in the way of expression. In addition, the folks themselves would be excited at the fact that their poor and rural life mean a lot to the educated elite and so give full cooperation.

The Challenges

The challenges facing oral literary teaching and research in Africa are quite numerous. It should be acknowledged that a number of African languages do not have published documentation of oral literature, thereby giving the erroneous impression of total absence of literary materials. So far, however, no society in Africa or anywhere else has been discovered, which, after thorough research, has been found to lack literature. The myth of a society without any literature, either oral or written, is as Andraejewak (1985) puts it 'a relic of the minimalistic attitudes towards non-literate societies', and especially to Africans which still persists.

Ruth Finnegan (1970) and Dorothy Blair (1970) have drawn attention to the factors that informed the retardation of studies in African oral literature. And as Clement Okafor (1980) rightly observes, 'by using African literature merely as illustration of various anthropological theories, the scholars in the area inadvertently created a climate which brought about the stunted growth of scholarly interest in African oral literature' (84). That oral literary scholarship is still passing through a growing process, is, as Okanlawon (1983) puts it, an indication of the fact that 'Africans relished in their oral literature without thinking of it as a subject or discipline and that the Europeans who introduced modern scholarship did not know at first that Africans had their own oral literature' (75).

Anene-Boyle (2002) has observed that 'a considerable number of otherwise competent ethnographic anthropological and linguistic works about Africa omit any references to the oral literature of the societies which they study' (12). Such omissions come about as a result of the fact that expatriate scholars who wrote such works did not have sufficient knowledge of the languages concerned.

In spite of teaching the subject for several decades, and the volume of writings that have poured into Africa on oral literature, academics have appeared reluctant to accord the status of literature to it until recently. It must be pointed out that the western world influenced this trend because of their long tradition of literate culture. Even after independence, the recognition did not come for a long time. For instance in Nigeria, until the early 1970s when the University of Ibadan started offering courses in oral literature in the department of English, no higher institution in Nigeria did so. Since then however, the number of African universities where oral literatures are researched into and taught as academic subjects has increased tremendously.

Another challenge facing oral literary teaching and research in Africa is the complexity of the definition of its boundaries. Oral literary materials are essentially the same for anthropology, folklore, oral history, traditional music and other components of oral tradition. Ikiddeh (1987) has argued that 'oral literature's interdisciplinary existence has further compounded the problem of working out a set of critical criteria that would help to distinguish it from other studies. In a spirited attempt at ensuring that oral literary scholarship takes its proper place, Ikiddeh quotes Kunene as urging the critic of oral literature to purge himself of western material for the criticism of African oral literature and embrace new tools. He explains that:

> A figure of speech is a term of avoidance… His (the poet's) use of figures of speech is in the artist's tradition. Factual reporting is the scientific way. But what the poet loses in scientific exactitude, he gains in aesthetic excellence. (136)

Prospects

While making a case for the survival of orality and oral literary research Finnegan (2005) posits that that there is not just one relation between the 'performed oral' and the 'textual written' neither is there a clear distinction

between them' (168). She argues that writing can interact with oral performance in many different ways. Such possibilities of interaction
include inter alia dictated transcription, performance score, memory cue,
hearing aid, notes for a speech, printed version of a memorized poem, a
tool for helping audiences understand a performance as it develops, and a
script for recreating and remembering a past performance. This multidimensional twist to the pursuit of oral scholarship makes Hearon's 2004
submission to the discourse significantly all-embracing. More so that it
brings to light the indispensable place of oral studies in biblical
discourse. According to him:

> What began some sixty years ago as an exploration of the oral tradition in
> the biblical text has brought us to a point where we now see our written
> remains as evidence of our oral-aural culture in which written and oral text
> and tradition were bound together in a dynamic relationship. This offers us
> opportunities to see and hear our written text in new ways: as patterns of
> sound beat in the task of persuasion in particular social historical contexts
> where performer and audience entered the world of the text in order to give
> meaning and power to a way of life. (Hearon 2004:103)

It is the submission of Wasamba (2005) that creates a safe landing for
our optimism. According to him:

> Oral literature in Africa continues to attract the interest of researchers
>
> and scholars because of its enduring aesthetic appeal and relevance. It
> reflects community life, the spirit of our ancestors and the process of
> development in our society. The texts come from the hearts, minds and
> memories of individual artists who are not just in touch with rural realities
> in their communities, but also the changing dynamics in the modern
> society. We know that some important traditional information or
> knowledge is not available in the classrooms and books. It is embedded in
> the hearts, minds and mouths of oral artists, traditional healers and com-
> munity leaders, waiting to be reactivated, performed, recorded, studied
> and perpetuated. The more we record, study and learn our oral literature,
> the more we understand ourselves and the less we are likely to recklessly
> ape foreign cultures. (1).

Conclusion

In conclusion, the discipline of oral literature has great prospects. Freed
from the fangs of misconception orchestrated by foreign scholars, and in
the light of the determination of the indigenous intellectuals and other
stakeholders of orality and performance literature to preserve the
African's cultural identity and thereby sustain the timelessness of our traditional value system, oral literary research in the continent, has a bright
future. And the teachers of oral literature are central to this revolution.
They have a responsibility, not only to develop passion for the subject
themselves, but also to ensure that their students are caught up in the

cultural revival. The young and potential scholars should be able to see their true essence in their oral traditions. At the lecture and tutorial levels, teachers should endeavour to be as practical and performance-driven as possible. All encouragement should also be given to students to carry out original fieldwork.

WORKS CITED

Abdulkadir Dandati 'Oral Composition: A Historical Appraisal', In Uchegbulam

Abalogun, Garba Ashiwaju and Regina Amadi-Ishiwala (eds.) *Oral Poetry in Nigeria* Nigeria Magazine 1981, 18-36.

Andrejeweski, B.W. and Pilaszewicz (eds) (1985) *Literature in African Languages: Theoretical Issues and Sample Surveys,* Cambridge: Cambridge University Press.

Anene-Boyle, F. A. (2002) .*Weaving the Tale:An Introduction to the Performance of Oral literature* Ibadan: Kraft Books Limited.

Bascom, William 'Folklore Research in Africa', *Journal of American Folklore,* Vol.77 No. 303, 1964, 12-13.

Blair, Dorothy *African Literature in French,* London: Cambridge University Press, 1970.

Dahle, Lars *Specimins of Malagasy Folk-Lore,* Antanarivo, 1877.

Finnegan Ruth *Oral Literature in Africa,* London: Oxford University Press, 1970.

—— (2005) 'The How of Literature' in *Oral Tradition.* 20/2, 164-187.

Frobenius, Leo *Atlantishe Goetterlarbe.* 1910,

Hearon, H.E. (2004) 'The Implication of 'Orality' for Studies of the Biblical Text' in *Oral Tradition* 19 No. 1.pp. 96-107.

Ikiddeh, Ime 'Two Decades of African Oral Literature: Towards the Formulation of Critical Standard in the Study of the Literature of Oral Expression' in R. Vanamali (ed.) *Critical Theory and African Literature,* Ibadan: Heinemann, 1987, 132-43.

Liyong, Taban Lo. (1972) *Popular Culture in East Africa.* Nairobi: East African Literature Bureau,

Okafor, Clement (1980) 'Research Methodology in African Oral Literature' in Chinua Achebe (ed.) *Okike: An African Journal of New Writing,* 16, 83-97.

Okanlawon, L.L.I. (1983) 'On the Problem of Oral Literature Research in Nigeria: The Position Today'in Uchegbulam Abalogun (ed.) *Nigeria Magazine* Lagos Nigeria, 73-84.

Okpewho, Isidore (1979) *The Epic in Africa: Toward a Poetics of the Oral Performance* New York: Columbia University Press.

—— 'The Anthropologist looks at Epic' in *Research in African Literatures,* Vol. 11, No. 4, 1980, 429-48.

—— 'Does Epic Exist in Africa?' in *Research in African Literatures,* Vol. 11, 1980, 308-26.

—— (1992) *African Oral Literature,* Indianapolis: Indiana University Press.

Wasamba, Peter 'Preservation of African Heritage through Research' in *The Nairobi Journal of Literature.* No. 3, March 2005.

Teaching & Reading
Doris Lessing's 'The Antheap'

Anne Serafin

'The Antheap' is a powerful story showing not only the relationship
between blacks and whites in Africa but also the power of art, of love, and
of power.' So wrote an eleventh grade Honors student, Ivan, a young man
of Russian descent and a talented artist. For many years, I assigned Doris
Lessing's early short story (or novella) 'The Antheap' to older high school
students – and later used it with adult discussion groups – sometimes in
conjunction with a current topic but often just as a striking and provocative story. Students in the United States learn a great deal about the Civil
Rights Movement and read literature by African-American writers, such
as Richard Wright, Langston Hughes, and Zora Neale Hurston. I aimed to
broaden their horizons further by providing information about a distant
part of the world. Through a story of two friends set in Southern Africa,
the students were able to analyze and discuss racial discrimination in
simple, human terms outside of their familiar political contexts. (Note:
the setting is not stated explicitly in the story but it is generally understood to be Southern Rhodesia where Doris Lessing lived as a child and
young woman.) This approach worked equally well with adults who
often came to the topic with greater political awareness than the high
school students but, as a result, possessed more firmly established beliefs
and attitudes. 'The Antheap' challenges preconceptions about loyalty,
responsibility, and generosity.

Lessing's novella is a perfect story in many ways: lengthy enough to
allow significant development of characters and events; plotted sufficiently to hold a reader's interest to the end; elliptical enough to pique
curiosity and raise questions. If one applies classic short story standards,
one character could be singled out as the protagonist, but Lessing weaves
two other important figures into the tapestry of the story. In addition, the
tale becomes highly charged regarding racial conflict and injustice, but
concludes with just the right portion of a 'happy ending'.

The trajectory of the story is unravelled by Ivan in a later section of his
reader response. 'I especially noticed that there were three separate yet
equally intricate societies in the story. The first was the antheap composed

80

of a community of blacks working together under the oppression of the British. The second consisted of the British schools which Tommy [a white child and the principal character] attended. The third was the hut [built atop a literal antheap] in which Tommy and Dirk [Tommy's mixed-race friend on the mine where they live] spend their vacations together. The hut was a sanctuary, an equilibrium of color and of viewpoints, a place where there was only love.' He continues to speculate about the text and builds to the eventual burning of the hut by the owner of the mine, Mr Macintosh. '[T]he burning of the hut was so destructive because it [the hut] was a union of color and Friendship ... a power place, a place of learning, culture and beauty.'

Meanwhile, as the plot unfolds, Lessing engages the reader with her signature descriptions of the physical landscape, in this case the mine property. One student wrote that she 'loved the description of the silence and noise that Tommy grew up in. In just a few sentences, the author conveyed the mood of Tommy's childhood.' A dramatic section from the text highlights these impressions:

> Tommy Clarke was three months when he came to the mine, and day and night his ears were filled with noise, every day and every night for years, so that he did not think of it as noise, rather, it was a different sort of silence. The mine-stamps thudded *gold*, gold, *gold*, gold, *gold*, gold, on and on, never changing, never stopping. So he did not hear them. But there came a day when the machinery broke, and it was when Tommy was three years old, and the silence was so terrible and so empty that he went screeching to his mother: 'It's stopped, it's stopped,' and he wept, shivering, in a corner until the thudding began again. (195-6)

Another student praised Lessing's descriptions because they helped her to 'visualize the setting' which drew her into the story. Further encomiums cited specific 'rich' [her word] descriptions: 'The mountains clench themselves into a fist here and the palm is a mile-wide reach of thick bush, where the heat gathers and clings' (191). But the student continues: 'The best description was of the mine, which was depicted as a beating heart. Everything around the mine was supported and kept alive by the mine.'

Analysis of the descriptive passages occurred regularly whenever I assigned the story. One student captured her reading experience thusly: 'As the story opened, the extensive description of the landscape went on for just the right amount of time. The description drew me into the story so that I was interested in the location where the story took place and what was going to occur. Then the plot started and I was hooked ... Lessing launched smoothly into the story.' Combining art and the landscape further strengthened the tale for her: 'I felt one of the best images in the book was of the carving Tommy did of the pit. 'Mr Macintosh saw the great pit, the black little figures tumbling and sprawling over into the flames, and he saw himself, stick in hand, astride on his two legs, at the edge of the pit, his hat on the back of his head' (234). This description perfectly embodies what the pit was ... a place of oppression for the blacks working there.'

These statements indicate some typical reactions when I have assigned 'The Antheap' to high school classes and adult groups. The story offers numerous possibilities for reflection and discussion. Teenagers would seem logical readers because of the ages of the main characters. Yet adults were once teenagers and so can reflect on their memories of adolescence with the benefit of distance. During one discussion, a man in the group, a psychologist, commented:

> Adolescent awakening and discovery stand out as a significant aspect of Doris Lessing's brilliant story 'The Antheap.' Two boys emerge as their own persons while essentially isolated from the world and the turmoil surrounding them. Despite the setting of Southern Africa and the vital issue of racial apartheid, the narrative operates as a study of adolescent male psyches. No matter the culture or geographical location, many developmental instincts and needs are common. The boys crave friendship, understanding and physical contact. Tommy, a privileged white boy, is almost wholly isolated from his nervous parents and the African community in which they reside. His primary champion is the white mine owner, whom he comes to despise. Dirk, seemingly an integral part of the black African society of the mine, turns out to be of mixed blood and the child of a fraught relationship. The boys bond – as two young people will do – and discover similar sensibilities and sensitivities, but invariably keep each other at a distance, as each adolescent searches for his personal identity.

Each age level responds according to its life perspective as well as its literary training. An adult woman in one of my groups wrote the following:

> In 'The Antheap,' Doris Lessing demonstrates an intimate understanding of both the physical beauties of the landscape of Southern Africa and the complexities of the region. In simple but affective words, Lessing draws the reader into the visual and aural world of a working gold mine. Then she allows readers to enter the private world of two young boys who live in continual proximity to the public chaos. Eventually, the narrator introduces the literal antheap of the title: as the boys build a hut on top of an African termite mound. But, in retrospect, one realizes that the gold mine constitutes an upside-down mirror of the anthill – a reverse antheap teeming with humans as frenetic as ants.

Adult readers also focused on the adult characters in Lessing's story to a greater extent than the students did: they brought experiential wisdom to the relationship between Tommy's parents as well as between the parents and their employer, and they offered a sympathetic understanding of Mr Macintosh's strengths as well as his obvious weaknesses.

An outstanding characteristic of this story is its holistic effect on readers. The individually successful components of a piece of writing are irrelevant if they do not meld into an effective whole. 'This story gripped firmly at the heart,' one high school student declared as he opened his essay on 'The Antheap.' Another student explained in her introduction that she'd read the story in one sitting and it held her attention all the way. 'The characters were completely realistic, and their interactions fit together so well that I never wondered if the story was farfetched.' Such powerful reactions dictate whether a written work (or any work of art) is worth evaluating further and the verdict has always been clear regarding this one.

One of the primary reasons I would assign the story would be to explore – through the personalities of well-limned characters – issues of racial mixing and injustice. When I first read 'The Antheap' and considered teaching it, I wondered whether the racial element was too obvious. One boy (Tommy) is from the white dominant culture; the other boy (Dirk) is of mixed blood from the oppressed majority. The boys play freely as children, but, as they grow, they are forced to recognize their differences and to separate for long periods until, eventually, they can only reunite clandestinely. I decided to venture into the story with a fairly mature eleventh grade class and, while a few students pronounced the story obvious or even trite, many revealed to me complexities I had not even thought of (and, as our discussions progressed, most of the original naysayers acknowledged a change in their attitudes). The students pointed out that the relationship between Tommy and Dirk became extremely charged and problematic as the boys grew older and as their society's attitudes impinged upon their originally spontaneous, mutual friendship. The story gains further complexity as Dirk's heritage becomes apparent: he is the unacknowledged son of the wealthy Scottish owner of the mine and for years, Mr Macintosh apparently had a sexual relationship with Dirk's mother. Information regarding the apartheid system of South Africa was always essential for classes, and discussions invariably raised the students' consciousness about this oppressive system. Many were motivated to ask, 'What can we do to change it?' With hindsight, we know that international awareness and pressure helped destroy the apartheid system and, while discrimination still exists in many places – at home and abroad – public protests can change laws and even societal attitudes; therefore, teaching a story involving social, cultural, and political issues can have extrinsic merit.

The students were given a brief introduction to the historical development of apartheid in South Africa and some regions of Southern Africa, and most had read Alan Paton's *Cry, the Beloved Country* in earlier classes. The adult readers had fuller knowledge of the geography, politics and history of the area and had read other texts, such as Doris Lessing's *The Grass Is Singing*, Nadine Gordimer's *July's People* and *A Sport of Nature*, Sindiwe Magona's *Living, Loving, and Lying Awake at Night* and *Mother to Mother*, and Zakes Mda's *The Madonna of Excelsior* and *The Heart of Redness*. No critical materials were assigned to any of the groups, though some sought information on their own and many of the adults had training in literary analysis. Lessing does not expatiate on racial issues or the apartheid system in her story; she reveals the injustices through the actions and reactions of the various characters. One high school student wrote eloquently on this topic:

> 'The Antheap' was fascinating because it revealed the responsibilities of white people in a society that oppresses blacks, even if one particular white person isn't an oppressor. It seems like there are a lot of African-American writers and activists who talk about the oppression of black people by white people, and my first reaction is often to say (or want to say) 'but *I* haven't done anything wrong.' Tommy seemed to understand the collective guilt of whites in his society without ever having it explained to him and – what was more impressive and interesting – he figured out one way to discharge some of his guilt. As [one of our classmates] said, he didn't do everything right, which makes his actions more valuable because they showed that taking responsibility isn't the same as being saintly – but he seemed to be, as far as Dirk was concerned, taking generally the right course of action.

The layers of human interaction created by Lessing evoked many such thoughtful responses. An effective story, such as this one, will inspire a level of discourse in keeping with the tenor of the text. Both high school students and adult readers spent considerable time digging deeply into the story. They examined Tommy's and Dirk's relationships with their families and with each other and, ultimately, Mr Macintosh's continued contacts with the African woman (notably unnamed) who is Dirk's mother.

As I continued to assign the story to classes, the topic of friendship was important. An innocent friendship between two children evolves into a complex, emotional, and sometimes physical struggle. The issues regarding friendship inevitably intertwine with the racial struggles in the story and a student in 2001 analyzed the complexities well:

> The most striking aspect of the story is Lessing's ability to show Tommy's conflicting emotions. Tommy is very much a three-dimensional character; at times he is angry because the white adults he knows treat blacks and coloreds as inferiors while at other times he fights with Dirk when Dirk mocks whites. Tommy truly struggles to maintain his dignity as a white person, but also to find dignity for Dirk. A less talented writer would have portrayed only one side of Tommy's character, either his desire to preserve the dignity of the title 'white' or his anger at whites' treatment of non-whites. Lessing, however, is able to show all of Tommy's emotions, making the story not only very realistic but also poignant and thought- provoking.

This friendship, however, can provide a haven for the boys from the pressures and corruption of their society. When they come together on Tommy's school holidays, their first response is often to fight. Standard criticism of the story often explores the possibility of these physical tussles as a manifestation of the budding sexuality of adolescent boys. In the classroom, though, it was simplest to gloss the battles – in the words of a student from 1997 – as 'an outlet for their anger about their racial frustrations.' Then, regarding the friendship that manages to survive severe challenges, the above student states: 'Even though Dirk and Tommy are boys of different cultures, they are willing to sacrifice their beliefs to remain friends. At seven years old, Tommy realizes that he should not associate with the black workers because white people believe they are better than blacks. Tommy, however, disobeys his parents' belief in white supremacy because Dirk is a friend regardless of his skin color.' Another student summarizes a general reaction that: 'The author uses the boys' friendship to demonstrate that racial tensions can be ameliorated by all people, if they are willing to understand and work through their differences. She shows that if two young boys can overcome their differences and learn to understand each other, then the white and black societies as a whole can do the same. The beautiful friendship which Lessing creates can make the reader examine his or her own views on racism, segregation, and discrimination.' What writer – or teacher selecting a story to read – could hope for more? Other compelling aspects of Lessing's story emerged during discussions. Tommy's artistic talents and efforts evoked both probing questions and incisive comments from many readers. Tommy's ability to recreate in wood his friend Dirk and others on the mine revealed a sensitivity in him beyond words or other actions. One student, who was also an artist, wrote 'I loved the descriptions of how he sculpted and painted, as if the images simply poured out of him and into whatever he was creating.' Debates raged widely about Tommy's sculpture of Dirk carved from a long piece of wood, leaving the lower half undefined. The narrator of 'The Antheap' states: 'Dirk's long, powerful body came writhing out of the wood like something struggling free. The head was clenched back, in the agony of the birth, eyes narrowed and desperate, the mouth ... tightened in obstinate purpose. The shoulders were free, but the hands were held; they could not pull themselves out of the dense wood, they were imprisoned. His body was free to the knees, but below them the human limbs were uncreated, the natural shapes of the wood swelled to the perfect muscled knees' (239). The narrative continues with, 'Mr Macintosh did not like it. He did not know what art was, but he knew he did not like this at all, it disturbed him deeply, so that when he looked at it he wanted to take an axe and cut it into pieces' (239). Such reactions were mirrored occasionally by high school students or adult readers – depending on their tastes in art and their understanding of the symbolism of Tommy's design. Frequent symbolic elements can be discerned in Lessing's story, and exploring the interpretive possibilities has provided some of the most enjoyable moments in discussions with all groups. Analyzing symbols always creates strong reactions, particularly among younger readers: some become excited by the search, almost as if they are embarking on a treasure hunt or detective probe; others become skeptical and might even accuse a teacher of going overboard in the discovery of symbols or of 'making up' all the meanings (which is, of course, what happens to a certain extent, but a teacher must insist that persuasive analysis be based on specific correlatives in a piece of literature). The antheap itself is the reigning symbol of the story. It possesses a binary identity that emerges gradually as the tale progresses. As the boys become older, Dirk builds a hut – a secret clubhouse where they can meet – on the top of a literal anthill in the bush away from the mine; here they renew and solidify their friendship after lengthy separations and make plans for their futures. Meanwhile, earlier in the story, the vast pit of Mr Macintosh's mine is described in terms analogous to an anthill. After numerous brief, glancing descriptions, the narrator finally becomes explicit: 'He [Tommy] went to the edge of the big pit and lay on his stomach looking down. ... Below, the great pit was so deep that the men working on the bottom of it were like ants. ... It was like an enormous ant-working, as brightly tinted as a fresh antheap' (199).

Before discussion of this topic can proceed, readers (young and old) often need to know what an African antheap looks like; most Americans can only envision the little mounds of sand with holes in the centre for ants to enter and exit found between the cracks in sidewalks. Pictures are extremely valuable to convince doubters that anthills in Africa can be large enough to support a small wooden hut, such as Dirk constructs. Then, as readers make connections backwards, they understand that the mine pit constitutes the reverse shape of the anthill. Teachers like to speak of 'Aha Moments' in a classroom setting, and often, at this juncture in discussions of Lessing's story, 'Aha' can truly be heard murmured in the room. Other symbols emerge as well and contribute to the development of the story. Early in the plot, Dirk, still a small child, finds a newborn duiker – a small African antelope – which Tommy buys from him; the animal, however, dies, despite Tommy's ardent ministrations during its brief illness. Also, the ants themselves can be an ambiguous symbol as they build and destroy almost simultaneously. The boys' shed represents many levels of meaning for the boys and for Mr Macintosh, who eventually destroys it. The money that Mr Macintosh bestows upon Tommy, whom he treats as a son – while ignoring his paternity of Dirk – can stand for a range of societal negotiations. The web of symbolism adds an intriguing dimension to what could otherwise be a straightforward, cautionary tale. In addition to all of these elements embedded in 'The Antheap,' the somewhat-happy-ending makes a positive contribution to the pantheon of literature selected by teachers. Students frequently complain that all the literature we assign is depressing or even tragic. So this story offers a variation from the common trend. Nevertheless, some readers object that the closing of 'The Antheap' is unrealistic or too pat. They say that Mr Macintosh would not be likely to agree to Tommy's terms regarding his education (which Mr Macintosh wants to pay for): Tommy demands that Dirk also be sent to university. Others express gratitude for the idea that holding courageously to one's beliefs can produce desirable results, albeit in a fictional representation. After this last conversation with the boys, Mr Macintosh, we are told, returns to his house 'an angry old man, defeated by something he did not begin to understand' (248). The story then concludes with the words: 'The victory was entirely theirs, but now they had to begin again, in the long and difficult struggle to understand what they had won and how they would use it' (403). Regarding this last statement, one young woman closed her essay with: 'I liked the ending because it combined victory, defeat and challenge, leaving things open rather than trying to conclude the entire story in one summarizing paragraph.' As satisfying as Lessing's resolution of the boys' dilemma can be, it thus opens the door to an uncertain future, a virtue as a teaching tool. The realism of the story lends itself to connecting the characters and political issues to 'real life' circumstances. In the discussions I have facilitated, both younger and older readers enjoy speculating about the challenges Tommy and Dirk will encounter as they head together to the university. Readers of different ages bring varied levels of knowledge and experience to such debates. 'The Antheap', as a whole, appeals to mature readers of all ages and provides sufficient complexity of plot motivation and decision-making so that each can respond according to his or her perceptions. A good story functions akin to an inkblot test, allowing readers to provide multiple interpretations. 'The Antheap' serves readers and teachers well in this regard; furthermore, it offers an engaging reading experience while teaching vital lessons of history and ethical behaviour.

WORKS CITED

Gordimer, Nadine. *July's People*, London: Penguin Books, 1981.
—— *A Sport of Nature*, Alfred A. Knopf, 1987.
Lessing, Doris. 'The Antheap' in *Five*. London: Panther Books, 1969 [reprinted 1974 (twice)].
Lessing, Doris. *The Grass Is Singing*. New York: Thomas Y. Crowell, 1950.
Mda, Zakes. *The Heart of Redness*. New York: Farrar, Strauss and Giroux, 2000.
—— *The Madonna of Excelsior*. New York: Farrar, Strauss and Giroux, 2002.
Paton, Alan. *Cry, the Beloved Country*. New York: Charles Scribener , 1949.

The Francophone Novel
of Africa & the Caribbean:
A Teacher's Perspective

Peter Wuteh Vakunta

Postcolonial Francophone literatures exist at the interface of French as a hegemonic language and its many regional variants that transform this corpus of writings into hybrid literature. Linguistic hybridity compounds the reading and teaching of Francophone literatures of Africa and the Caribbean. An incontrovertible manifestation of linguistic variance in contemporary Francophone literatures is the tendency on the part of fiction writers to resort to modes of writing characterized by linguistic indigenization – an attempt to appropriate the language of the ex-colonizer. The Francophone novel, in particular, has been described by literary critics as a multi-layered text engendered by a plurality of 'voices' and the multicultural contexts from where the text takes root. Franco-phone novelists tend to create hybrid texts that demand of readers to be not just bilingual but also bicultural. Thus, these texts tend to be not only sites for the negotiation of cultural spaces but also loci where writers resort to linguistic resistance in order to call into question some assumptions associated with colonialism, neo-colonialism, and imperialism. In this paper I contend that the Francophone novel of Africa and the Caribbean can no longer be taught using the same paradigms that are used in teaching metropolitan French novels, the more so because African and Caribbean Francophone writers continually resort to a multiplicity of dialectal forms of French as tools of communication.

This paper provides answers to the following intriguing questions, namely: What are some of the textual and extra-textual considerations that instructors of the Francophone novel of Africa and the Caribbean must reckon with in their attempt to comprehend the form and content of indigenous stories written in French? What is the nature of the translation process that takes place in Francophone novels? What pedagogical frame-works are suitable for teaching this kind of literature? Recourse to the French language in writing indigenous literatures harbours problems of its own. Though developed to express and reflect European worldviews, imagination and sensibilities, Francophone writers from Africa, and the Caribbean tend to tinker with the French language in a bid to convey messages that seem at variance with its native traditions. In this vein, these writers find themselves writing in a language they wish to deconstruct in order to make it bear the imprint of their socio-cultural realities. This task is accomplished through the process of linguistic indigenization, a process that enables creative writers to transpose the imagination, worldview and cultural peculiarities of indigenous peoples into metropolitan French. Arguing along similar lines, Chantal Zabus (1991) observes that the concept of indigenization translates 'the writer's attempt at textualizing linguistic differentiation and conveying African concepts, thought patterns and linguistic concepts through the ex-colonizer's language' (23). African and Caribbean Francophone writers tend to appropriate the French language by having recourse to discursive strategies that transgress the canons of hexagonal French – semantic shift, intralingual translation, loan translation, lexical interpolation, vernacular transcription and more.

The rationale for resorting to linguistic appropriation goes beyond the simple need to provide works of fiction with a cultural basis and aesthetic value. Oftentimes, Francophone writers resort to appropriative techniques out of a genuine need to communicate effectively as we will see in the literary analysis below. Here then is a literature whose writers depend heavily on translation as a literary canon. The term 'translation' should not be understood to refer to the inter-lingual communicative process of replacing a text in the source language by a lexically equivalent text in the target language. When Francophone writers resort to translation as a literary device they do not act in the technical capacity of a text processor engaged in the simple conversion of words and sentences in the source text into equivalent words and sentences in the target language. To put this differently, writers do not simply take words in the indigenous language for which they look for equivalents in French. Writers who resort to translation as a creative writing device seem to be involved in a conscious act of intra-lingual translation that enables them to transpose the worldview and imagination of indigenous peoples into the French language. Ahmadou Kourouma, who has distinguished himself as a linguistic innovator, makes it abundantly clear that what he did in writing *Les soleils des indépendances* (1970) was not a mechanical process of replacing Malinke words with their French equivalents:

> It is not translation from Malinke...I thought in Malinke and then tried to present things the way a Malinke would see them; the way they would come to his mind. It is not a translation from Malinke. (Badday, 1970: 12)

In my attempt to shed light on the problematic of language choice in the Francophone novel of Africa and the Caribbean, I selected a corpus comprising Ahmadou Kourouma's *Les soleils des indépendances* (1970), Chamoiseau's *Texaco* (1992), Patrice Nganang's *Temps de chien* (2001), Mercédès Fouda's *Je parle camerounais* (2001), and Gabriel Fonkou's *Moi*

Taximan (2001). These novels constitute a watershed in the evolution of the Francophone novel. The publication of these texts marks the dawn of a new era characterized by writers' unbridled inclination toward the subversion of French grammatical canons as the 'Empire writes back' to borrow words from Ashcroft et al. (1989). Kourouma's peculiar style of writing labelled the 'malinkelization' of French is distinctive by the writer's recourse to semantic shifts, vernacular transcriptions, phrasal restructuring and more. 'Malinkelization'[1] of French in *Les soleils* begins right from the title of the novel. The expression 'les soleils' is a calque on the Malinke discursive mode. The word 'soleil' has to be put back into the Malinke cultural context in order to discern its full signification. The Malinke use 'soleil' to designate a time-frame ('season' and by extension, an 'era'). It is in this sense that Kourouma's narrator talks of 'les soleils des indépendances' (7-8, 15,141) [the suns of independences][2]; 'les soleils de Samory' (142) [the suns of Samory]; 'les soleils des Toubabs' (142), [the suns of the Whites]; and 'les soleils du parti unique' (141) [the suns of one-party politics].   The pluralization of the word 'soleils' derives from Malinke worldview. Its signification may not be obvious to a non-Malinke reader on account of cultural unfamiliarity. Sensing the ambiguity in the title, Kourouma comes to the assistance of the reader with a translation: 'l'ère des indépendances' (7) [the Era of Independence]. Through the technique of semantic shift, Kourouma introduces a troublesome element into standard French. What Kourouma does in *Les soleils* is not the mechanical translation activity of replacing Malinke words with their French language equivalents. Rather, he thinks in Malinke and then imagines how best to render his mode of thought in the French language. The equivalence he seeks is semantic rather than formalistic. The literary canon of 'malinkelization'could impede the comprehension and teaching of this novel, especially if the instructor is not conversant with some of culture-specific tropes that Kourouma uses in his narrative.

In a similar vein, linguistic indigenization fulfills the critical function of cross-cultural communication in Fouda's *Je parle camerounais*. Fouda makes abundant use of Camfranglais[3] expressions in her attempt to transpose the modes of speech of Cameroonians into written French. An understanding of the contexts in which Camfranglais expressions and other Camerounsimes[4] are used in Fouda's novel would not only facilitate readers' comprehension of the text but would also make it possible for literature instructors to analyze the circumstances surrounding its creation. Fouda often spices her narrative with expressions that may be incomprehensible to people outside the closed circle of Camfranglais speakers as the following example shows: 'Si depuis belle lurette vous vous démenez de-ci de-là sans trouver aucune occasion à saisir sur le plan matériel, vous pourrez toujours vous plaindre que le dehors est dur...' (5).[5] 'Le dehors est dur' is a Cameroonianism that conveys the idea that times are tough. Loan words gleaned from Cameroonian culinary register are employed frequently in *Je parle camerounais* for the purpose of effective communication. When the central character tells another character in the novel: 'votre estomac vous lance des insultes' (9)[6], he is insinuating that that the interlocutor is terribly hungry and should go and fetch some food to eat without further delay. Fouda draws readers' attention to the fact that working-class Cameroonians eat their lunch in makeshift open-air restaurants called 'tournedos' [roadside restaurants] erected on the sidewalk as seen in this excerpt: 'Vous avez alors la possibilité d'aller manger au tournedos. Ne vous réjouissez pas trop vite! Vous n'irez que dans l'un de ces restaurants de plein air, faits de bancs et de tables assemblés, et où, tout bêtement, le client tourne le dos à la route!'(10)[7] 'Tourne-dos' has no equivalent in standard French because the reality does not exist in the French socio-cultural context. This cultural vacuum needs to be filled by teachers of this novel by resorting to near-equivalents in metropolitan French if possible.

By 'Cameroonizing' standard French, Fouda distances herself from speakers of standard French by underscoring the 'Africanness' of the French she writes. Her text is replete with Cameroonian turns of phrase as this other example shows: 'J'ai seulement un 'papa-j'ai grandi' et les 'sans confiance'' (37).[8] A 'papa-j'ai grandi' is a pair of pants that appears too short or too small for the wearer because s/he has grown bigger. Cameroonians often employ this sort of expression as a form of mockery and as a reminder to the person wearing the pants that it is time to buy a new one. 'Sans confiance' is an expression used by Camanglophones to describe low quality rubber-made flipflops whose strings can snap without warning. The word formation technique called 'compounding' is another word literary device employed judiciously by Fouda with the intent of transposing Cameroonian socio-cultural experiences into the French language. She creates compound words by combining words from various native languages spoken in Cameroon. Examples include: 'Mamie Koki' (10)[9], 'Mamie Ndolè' (10)[10], and 'Mamie Atchomo' (10)[11]. The word 'mamie' is the Pidgin equivalent of the standard French 'mère'[12]. 'Koki', 'ndolè', and 'atchomo' are local Cameroonian dishes cherished by Cameroonian youngsters. Cameroonian youths often address older women as 'mamie' as a gesture of respect due to age. In the commercial arena, this term is used in reference to a woman from whom a client buys food on a regular basis as the following excerpt shows: 'Au tournedos, officie l'asso, diminutive flatteur de 'associé (e), est cette personne chez qui vous faites régulièrement des achats et qui, lorsque c'est fort sur vous, vous fait manger un crédit...' (10)[13] 'Manger un crédit' translates the standard French expression 'acheter à crédit' [buy on credit]. The word 'manger' has been given a different signification in Fouda's text. 'Manger' (to eat) could be translated as 'acheter' (to buy) in this context. Semantic reconstruction is a literary device widely used by Fouda for the purpose of communicative effectiveness. However, literature instructors need to pay particular attentions to this 'word smiting' (the process used by African writers to create words to convey their imagination, thought processes and cultural peculiarities) because words can harbour latent meanings. A superficial reading of Fouda's text would do a great disservice to students of the novel.

In *Je parle camerounais,* Fouda deliberately endows the French language with a local flavour and aesthetic as the following example illustrates: 'Attisé ainsi, vous seriez ridicule, et Max a bien raison une fois de plus de montrer ses 'attrape-manioc': il se moque gentiment de vous.' (36)[14]. Les 'attrape-manioc' is a metaphorical expression used in reference to human teeth. This neologism derives from the fact the staple food of Fouda's people is manioc (cassava). 'Attraper le manioc avec ses dents' is to 'eat a meal of cassava'. Usage of this kind lends credibility to the fact that the French language in Fouda's novel has been doctored to reflect Cameroonian socio-cultural realities. A non-Cameroonian teaching this text is likely to draw a blank on account of the preponderance of Cameroonian speech patterns and lexical items in the narrative.

Fouda's *Je parle camerounais* is only one out of many Francophone so-called 'new' novels written in a peculiar style. In *Temps de chien* (2001) Patrice Nganang makes abundant use of code-switching as a narrative paradigm. *Temps de chien* addresses the problematic of language choice in Francophone literatures beyond the Hexagon. Nganang's text provides answers to the question relating to how Francophone Africans should tell their own stories. He teases out the space between the writer's mother tongue and what s/he writes in a 'loan' language. In his attempt to transpose the speech mannerisms of Cameroonians into written French, Nganang uses the technique of code-switching. *Temps de chien* is written in an amalgam of codes – French, Pidgin English, Camfranglais and numerous indigenous languages. It is a text in which street-talk, also known as 'Kam-Tok', 'Camspeak' or 'Majunga Talk' (Ze Amvela, 56) blends freely with conventional French to produce a new code whose effect on the reader is not only exhilarating but also enriching. Our reading of *Temps de chien* focuses on how the novelist uses linguistic innovation not only as a narrative technique but also as a tool of resistance as this example clearly shows: 'Ma woman no fit chasser me for ma long dis-donc! Après tout, ma long na ma long!'(80). The translator did a laudable job of translating this urban slang into English as follows: 'My woman can't throw me out of my house, I tell you! After all, my house is my house!'(208) The signifier 'long' means 'home' in Camfranglais. The translator uses the same technique to translate the following passage: 'La voix d'un lycéen lui disait: comme d'habitude, Mama Mado. Et ma maîtresse connaissait son goût. La voix d'un autre exigeait, put oya soté, for jazz must do sous-marin.' (84).[15] The term 'oya' is a Pidgin English word for 'oil', in this case oil used in cooking. 'Jazz' is a slang word for 'beans', and 'jazz sous-marin' could be translated as 'beans submerged in oil'. Cameroonians use this expression to describe the trumpet-like sound that one's stomach would make if one ate badly cooked beans. These examples serve to underscore the fact that code-switching is used as an effective weapon of resistance in *Temps de chien*. At the same time, it is a literary device that could complicate the task of teaching the novel. This holds true for Gabriel Fonkou's *Moi Taximan* where Camfranglais and vernacular language expressions abound.

Moi Taximan is replete with French words that have undergone semantic transformation as seen in the following excerpt: 'Je ne mangeais chez moi que le soir, sauf les jours où je me faisais aider par un 'attaquant'...afin de me reposer un peu.'(18)[16] The narrator employs the word 'attaquant' to describe a taxi driver who not only works overtime but is often aggressive and prone to road rage. One other example that illustrates Fonkou's verbal sophistry is the following: 'On sortait de l'opération avec un plus grand sourire si, en plus, les passagers longue distance avaient 'proposé'...' (8)[17] A little further, the narrator sheds ample light on the signification of the word 'proposé': '... payer plus cher que le tarif normal' (8)[18]. Fonkou's neologisms shed light on the mindset of his characters: 'Entre deux clients, Justine et sa mère participaient activement à l'entretien de la chaude ambiance du secteur des 'bayam sellam': potins, querelles simulées, plaisanteries et fausses confidences bruyantes y provoquaient de gros éclats de rire.' (131).[19] The term 'Bayam sellam', is derived from Cameroonian Creole, also called Pidgin English. Literally, it means 'buy them sell them'. It is used in this novel to describe market women whom the protagonist describes as 'des revendeuses, cette catégorie de commerçantes aggressives sans les lesquelles nos marchés perdraient leur âme' (130).[20] 'Bayam sellam' trade is a vital economic activity in the informal sector born out of dire need (the struggle to improve the livelihood of individuals and families).

Some lexical items in *Moi Taximan* are English language words that have been endowed with new meanings as this example shows: 'Au bout de la journée le plus souvent chacun de nous affichait un sourire de contentement et nous nous quittions à la nuit tombante sur de vigoureuses poignées de mains prolongées par un 'toss'...'(13).[21] Fonkou's protagonist defines the term 'toss' as 'salut du bout des pouces et des majeurs entrecroisés puis séparés dans un vif frottement sonore' (13).[22] The English language has enriched Cameroonian literature of French expression as seen in the following statement: 'La journée d'hier a été djidja' (19)[23]. 'Djidja', loanword from Pidgin English, derives from the English word 'ginger'. Camanglophones use this culinary term to describe a difficult situation comparable to what hexagonal French speakers would describe as 'une mer à boire' [an uphill task]. From the pedagogical perspective, this sort of linguistic jugglery does not make matters easy for instructors who have to devise appropriate paradigms for literary interpretation.

Oftentimes, Fonkou's characters draw attention to ethnic dichotomy and its social ramifications in Cameroon as this example illustrates: 'Je ne sais rien, espèce de Bami' (24)[24]. The word 'Bami' is an abbreviation of 'Bamileke', one of the ethnic groups in Cameroon loathed by other Cameroonians for their ruthless money-mongering and resourceful mindset. Used the way Fonkou does in this text, the word harbours derogatory undertones. As these examples illustrate, neology is a technique constantly exploited by Fonkou to create new words that portray the prism through which he perceives social reality. He makes ingenious use of the technique of linguistic innovation to portray both the impact of the socio-cultural realities of Cameroon on creative writing as well as the significant influence of language choice on postcolonial fictional writing. Fonkou mixes languages purposefully in a bid to under-score the polyglossic context from which his text sprouts as this example illustrates: 'La plus grosse surprise se situa le dimanche où la réunion des femmes de mon village vint laver l'enfant' (186).[25] 'Laver l'enfant' is a native tongue expression that describes the cultural ritual during which the birth of a baby is celebrated by family members. In Fonkou's native language, this ritual is called 'le yaal, à la fois danse et chants pour célébrer la naissance de l'enfant' (187)[26]. The need to possess both trans-lingual and transcultural competences in order to successfully teach this novel is made all the more evident through the use of culture-specific expressions to portray indigenous mores as seen in the examples discussed above.

The beauty of indigenization as a tool of literary creativity is that it cuts across the entire Francophone world. Linguistic manipulation is increa-singly becoming a popular mode of writing in Caribbean Francophone literature as seen in the following excerpt culled from Patrick Chamoiseau's seminal novel *Texaco* (1992):

> Je vendis les cocos du pied-coco de Pè-Soltene, un vieux nègre-distillerie qui fumait sa vieillesse sous ce seul arbre planté. Je vendis des crabes que j'allais déterrer sur les terres de Dillon. Je vendis des bouteilles et des casseroles anglaises. Je vendis des fiasques à parfum qu'une pacotilleuse ramenait d'Italie. Ces djobs me procuraient des sous que je serrais comme ceux de Nelta (après avoir payé notre huile, notre sel, notre pétrole, un bout de toile, et cotisé, comme toutes les bonnes gens d'En-ville à la société mutualiste', L'humanité Solidaire. (299)[27]

Translators of *Texaco* did a laudable job of preserving the cultural flavour of the source text in the English language translation. Their rendition of the compound noun 'Pe-Soltène' as 'Pa Soltène' is culturally significant. The word 'Pè' is a Creole word derived from the French word 'Père'. 'Pe' is probably a contraction of the French word 'père' [father]. Chamoiseau's translators did an excellent job of finding a culturally relevant equivalent in the target language. 'Pa' appears to be a contraction of the word 'Papa'. The literary significance of this word choice resides in the fact that Chamoiseau succeeds in conveying the cultural implication of the Creole word 'Pè' in the French language. In Black communities, 'Pè' does not necessarily translate the notion of filial relationship between speaker and interlocutor. Rather, it is a term of respect used by youths in addressing people of a ripe age. Indeed, it is a marker of age difference. Another noteworthy instance of linguistic appropriation in this novel is the writer's choice of the word 'djobs. The word is probably a derivation from the English word 'job'. It is a transcription of the way Creole speakers would oralize the word in daily discourse.

What makes Chamoiseau's narrative style both interesting and challenging for students and instructors of Francophone Caribbean literature is the fact that he blends together standard French, Martinican regional French, Creole, and his own creative wordplay in order to give esthetic value to his novel. He seems to have a predilection for inventing an original style of writing which critics have dubbed the 'chamoisification' of the French language. Chamoisification aptly describes Chamoiseau's wordplay in fictional writing; his attempt to transpose Creole identity into his works. His subversion of the ex-colonizer's language amounts to a differential discourse that serves as a response to colonial elaboration of authority and forced subjugation. His re-articulation of Caribbean identity (*antillanité*)[28] is discernible in the manner in which he blends creolized and hexagonal variants of French in his text. The concept of 'chamoisification' of French is of special interest to us given that it underscores the novelist's quest for a third code – a personalized writing mode quite distinct from that employed by Metropolitan French writers. In Chamoiseau's novel, standard and nonstandard forms come together on the same page and wrestle with each other for control of the narrative, just as they are jostling for power and prestige within the Martinican society itself. Commenting on his style of writing in an interview he granted Marie-Jose N'Zenou Tayo, Chamoiseau asserts that it was ' ni un français créolisé, ni un créole francisé, mais un français chamoisisé' (155)[29]. Instructors encountering Chamoiseau's texts for the first time will have to do their homework in order to decipher the signification of the various culture-specific rhetorical devices that the writer employs for the purpose of self-expression. Chamoiseau's language mixing is challenging because readers find themselves looking for meanings of words and expressions and stopping to digest unfamiliar sentences again and again. The use of code-switching compounds is an initial frustration but over time ideas surface and it becomes more comfortable. Chamoiseau achieves his objective of showing the historical and social complexities of language usage in Caribbean literature.

If up to a certain point, each postcolonial writer has to reinvent language, the situation of Francophone writers outside France is peculiar in that for them, French is an occasion for constant mutations and modifications. Engaged as they are in the game of language, these writers have to 'manufacture' their own language of fiction, in a multilingual context often affected by signs of polyglossia. Contemporary Francophone literatures exist at the crossroads of languages and cultures. Incontrovertible evidence of alterity in this new form of literature can be found in the emergence of modes of writing distinguished by their nonconformity to linguistic norms. In his text *The Francophone African Text: Translation and the Postcolonial Experience* (2006), Gyasi observes that Francophone fiction writers create 'French that is in consonance with the new African environment and the characters that live in it....' (77). He describes this inclination on the part of writers as an act of defiance. As the foregoing analysis suggests, emerging African and Caribbean novels of French expression qualify to be categorized as hybrid texts engendered by the plurality of 'voices', and the multilingual contexts of creativity. Francophone fiction writers create multi-faceted texts which demand that readers be both multilingual and multicultural in order to be able to unravel the hidden textual significations. The texts examined in this paper function as sites of cultural and linguistic negotiation.

In conclusion, the intent of this paper has not been simply to provide you with information on the plethora of modes of writing that exist in Francophone African and Caribbean literatures. The intent has been to aid professors of Francophone literatures, in their reflections on the nature of the texts they teach semester after semester, and propose pedagogical paradigms suitable for teaching such literatures. The question that begs to be asked at this juncture is why it is critical for instructors of Francophone novels of Africa and the Caribbean to be conversant with the evolutionary trends inherent in these texts? I maintain that knowledge of the French language alone will not suffice to do justice to the teaching of the novels discussed in this paper. Teachers of Francophone novels cannot but be like the texts they teach – at once bilingual and bicultural. Given the polytonality and multi-cultural composition of Francophone novels of Africa and the Caribbean, instructors must conceive appropriate literary models for teaching these texts. The texts analyzed in this paper irrefutably call for multifaceted frameworks for instruction three of which I discuss below.

1 *Critical Thinking Culture-Based Model*

This instructional model is based on Bloom's Taxonomy (1956) of textual analysis. To effectively communicate the holistic message embedded in the essential elements of information (EEI's) in a text, Bloom argues, instructors need to create learning tasks that enable learners to interact with texts at six different cognitive levels: *Evaluation* (making value decisions about issues, resolving controversies, assessing theories, composing ideas, evaluating outcomes); *Synthesis* (creating a unique original product that may be in verbal form or a combination of ideas to

form a new whole, using old concepts to create new ones); *Analysis* (organizing ideas and recognizing trends, finding the underlying structure of
communication, identifying motives); *Application* (using and applying
knowledge, problem-solving, use of facts and principles); *Comprehension* (interpreting, translating from one medium to the other, demon-
strating, summarizing, discussing the signifier and signified); *Knowledge*
(recall of information, discovery, and observation).

2 Hermeneutic (Exegetic) Model

The theory of hermeneutics or exegesis propounded by Schleiermacher
and Bowie (1998) underscores the importance of interpreting, not only the
latent (hidden) meanings embedded in a literary text but also the situational dimensions that constitute the matrix in which the text was written.

He further underscores the need to use the hermeneutic circle in the
process of unravelling the significations contained in the deep structure
of a literary text. The hermeneutic circle facilitates the analysis of a
literary text by enabling readers to come to grips with the fact that one's
understanding of the text as a whole is established by reference to the
individual parts. Schleiermacher further notes that neither the whole text
nor any individual part can be understood without reference to one
another, and hence, it is a circle. The circularity inherent in hermeneutics
implies that the meaning of a text is to be found within its cultural, historical, and literary contexts.

3 Styles- and Strategies-Based Instruction (SSBI)

Cohen and Weaver (2006) conceived the Styles- and Strategies-Based
Instructional model as a framework for teaching foreign languages. It is very
suitable for teaching literatures written in foreign languages. The framework is based on the theory of scaffolding, a concept that stems from the
idea that at the beginning of the learning process, learners need a great deal
of support; gradually, this support is taken away to allow students to
develop a sense of independence. This is what Cohen and Weaver call the
gradual release of responsibility. Other facets of the model include:
modelling, cooperative learning, activation of prior knowledge, student
learning choices and self-initiated learning. The SSBI is a learner-focused
approach that explicitly encourages different kinds of intervention in the
classroom. Emphasis is placed on how specific learning tasks might call for
certain learning style preferences and call for certain teaching strategies.

In a nutshell, by revisiting seminal novels written by Kourouma,
Fouda, Nganang, Fonkou and Chamoiseau, I sought to undercore the fact
that African and Caribbean novels of French expression are, in essence,
hybrid texts that may defy superficial reading. Literary indigenization is

not an oddity; rather is a timely response to the call for new ways of writing Francophone so-called 'new' novels. Teachers of Francophone literatures of Africa and the Caribbean cannot continue to teach these texts using the same models that were used in teaching metropolitan French novels like *Madame Bovary* (Flaubert, 1856); *Le rouge et le noir* (Stendhal, 1830); *Germinal* (Zola,1885); *L'immoraliste* (Gide,1902); *La jalousie* (Robbe-Grillet,1957); *Planétarium* (Sarraute,1959) and so on. Whether or not the novelists included in our corpus have achieved the goal of de-Europeanizing their novels is a question that falls beyond the scope of this paper. Literary scholars like Ngugi wa Thiong'o in 1986 have argued that to qualify as indigenous, African literatures have to be written in native languages. He further points out that 'Literature written by Africans in European languages ... can only be termed Afro-European literature; that is, the literature written by Africans in European languages' (27). Much as we salute the success of the aforementioned novelists in imprinting their texts with the worldview, imagination, speech mannerisms, and cultural characteristics of indigenous peoples, we cannot lose sight of the fact the core of these texts is written in French, a European language. In spite of the impressive linguistic innovations inherent in them, they are still essentially French language novels. For these writers, French is a necessary evil with which they must come to terms.   Straddling two cultural spheres, Kourouma, Fouda, Nganang, Fonkou and Chamoiseau find themselves at the crossroads of languages. They cannot be faithful to the one without betraying the other.

NOTES

1 Transposition of Malinke thought patterns and worldview into French.
2 All translations are mine unless otherwise indicated.
3 Camfranglais is a 'composite language consciously developed by secondary school pupils who have in common a number of linguistic codes, namely French, English and a few widespread indigenous languages'(Kouega, 23).
4 Cameroonianisms.
5 If you have been searching here and there in vain for a job to make ends meet, you could always complain that times are tough.
6 Your stomach is shouting insults at you.
7 You now have the opportunity to go eat in a roadside restaurant. Don't be too excited! You will go to one of these makeshift restaurants in the open air, where benches and tables are assembled for clients to sit and sheepishly turn their backs to the street!
8 I only have a 'Papa-I-have-grown-up and a pair of 'sans kong'.
9 Mama Koki.
10 Mama Ndolè.
11 Mama Atchomo.
12 Mother.
13 At the roadside restaurant, you'd find the asso, term of flattery that describes the woman from whom you buy food regularly, and who would allow you eat

on credit when times are tough.

14 Dressed up in this manner, you'd look ludicrous, and Max, once again, would have cause to expose his 'cassava-traps'. He's discreetly making fun of you.

15 A student's voice would say, the usual, Mama Mado, and my mistress knew just what he wanted. Another's voice would order, put oya soté, for jazz must do sous-marin (*Dog Days*, 57).

16 I only ate at home in the evening, except on days when I had asked an 'attacker' to replace me so that I could have some rest.

17 At the end of the day, we returned home with a big smile if, in addition to the normal fare, long-distance commuters had proposed.

18 Paying more than the normal fare.

19 Between two customers, Justine and her mother took part in the heated discussions that animated the 'bayam sellam' section of the market: gossip, fake quarrels, jokes and noisy false pretences that caused outbursts of laughter.

20 Retail traders, this category of aggressive market women without whom our markets would lose their vivacity.

21 More often than not, at the end of the day, each one of us wore a smile of contentment as we parted at nightfall, vigorously shaking hands and saying 'toss'.

22 Handshake with the tips of the thumb and middle-fingers intertwined, followed by a quick separation and loud sound.

23 Yesterday was djidja.

24 I have no clue, you Bami fellow.

25 The biggest surprise came on a Sunday, the day when the association of women from my village came to wash the baby.

26 The yaal – song and dance that celebrate the birth of a child.

27 I sold the coconuts from the tree of Pa Soltene, an old distillery-blackman who smoked away his old-age under his only tree. I sold crabs which I'd dig up on Dillon's lands. I sold bottles and saucepans. I sold perfume flasks that a trinket merchant brought from Italy. These odd jobs brought me money that I (after having paid for the oil, salt, kerosene, a piece of cloth, donated a bit like all of City's good people to the mutual aid society, Human Solidarity) kept like Nelta did (*Texaco*, 272).

28 A literary and political movement developed in the 1960s that stresses the creation of a specific West Indian identity out of a multiplicity of ethnic and cultural elements.

29 Neither creolized French nor Frenchified Creole; rather Chamoisified French.

BIBLIOGRAPHY

Achebe, Chinua. *Things Fall Apart*. London: Heinemann, 1958.

Anderson, Lorin, David Krathwohl, and Peter Airasian. *Taxonomy of Learning, Teaching and Assessing: A Revision of Bloom's Taxonomy of Educational Objectives*. New York: Longman, 2001.

Aschcroft, Bill, Gareth Griffiths, Helen Tiffin. eds, *The Empire Writes Back: Theory and Practice in Post-colonial Literatures*. London and NewYork: Routledge, 1989.

Badday, Moncef S. 'Ahmadou Kourouma, écrivain ivoirien.' *L'Afrique littéraire et Artistique* 10 (1970):8-19.

Bloom. B.S. *Taxonomy of Educational Objectives*. New York : David McKay Co. Inc., 1956.

Boni, Nazi. *Crépuscule des temps anciens.* Paris: Présence Africaine, 1962.

Chamoiseau, Patrick. *Texaco.* Paris: Gallimard, 1992.

Cohen, Andrew and Susan Weaver. *Styles-and Strategies-Based Instruction: A Teacher's Guide.* Minneapolis: University of Minnesota, CARLA, 2006.

Flaubert, Gustave. *Madame Bovary.*[1856] Paris: Garnier, 1971.

Fonkou, Gabriel K. *Moi Taximan.* Paris: L'Harmattan, 2001.

Fouda Mercédès. *Je parle camerounais: pour un renouveau francofaune.* Paris: Karthala, 2001.

Gassama, Makhily. *La Langue d'Ahmadou Kourouma ou le français sous le soleil d'Afrique.* Paris: Karthala, 1995.

Gide, André. *L'immoraliste.* Paris: Mercure de France, 1902.

Gyasi, Kwaku, A. *The Francophone African Text: Translation and the Post-colonial Experience.* New York: Peter Lang, 2006.

Koné, Amadou. *Du récit oral au roman: étude sur les avatars de la tradition héroïque sur le roman africain.* Abidjan: CEDA, 1985.

Kouega, Jean-Paul. 'Camfranglais: A New Slang in Cameroonian Schools.' *English Today* 19.2 (2003): 23-29.

Kourouma, Ahmadou. *Les soleils des indépendances.* Paris: Editions du Seuil, 1970.

—— *The Suns of Independence.* Trans. Adrian Adams. NewYork: Africana, Publications, 1981.

Millogo, Louis. *Nazi Boni premier écrivain du Burkina Faso: la langue bwamu dans Crépuscule des temps anciens.* Limoges: Presses universitaires de Limoges, 2002.

Ngalasso, Mwatha Musangi. 'De *Les soleils des indépendances* à *En attendant le vote des bêtes savages*: quelles évolutions de la langue chez Ahmadou Kourouma? *Littératures francophones: langues et style.* Paris: L'Harmattan (2001): 13-47.

Nganang, Patrice. *Temps de chien.* Paris: Serpent à Plumes, 2001.

—— *Dog Days.* Trans. Amy Baram Reid. Charlottesville: University of Virginia Press, 2001.

Ngugi wa Thiong'o. *Decolonising the Mind: the Politics of Language in African Literature.* London: James Currey, 1986.

Obiechina, Emmanuel. *Culture, Tradition and Society in the West African Novel.* Cambridge: Cambridge University Press, 1975.

Okara,Gabriel. *The Voice.* London: A. Deutsch, 1964.

Robbe-Grillet, Alaine. *La jalousie.* Paris: Editions de Minuit, 1957.

Sarraute, Nathalie. *Planétarium.* Paris: Gallimard, 1959.

Scheub, Harold. 'A Review of African Oral Traditions and Literature.' *African Studies Review* 28.2-3 (1985): 1-72.

Schleiermacher, Friedrick and Andrew Bowie. *Hermeneutics and Criticism : And Other Writings.* Cambridge : Cambridge University Press, 1998.

Soubias, Pierre. 'Deux langues pour un texte: problèmes de style chez Ahmadou Kourouma.' *Champs du signe* 5 (1995): 209-202.

Stendhal. *Le rouge et le noir.* [1830] Paris: Larousse, 1972.

Tutuola, Amos. *The Palm-Wine Drinkard.* London: Faber and Faber, 1952.

Zabus, Chantal. *The African Palimpsest: Indigenization of Language in the West African Europhone Novel.* Amsterdam: Rodopi, 1991.

Ze Amvela, Etienne. 'Reflexions on the Social Implications of Bilingualism in the Republic of Cameroon.' *Annals of the Faculty of Letters and Social Sciences.* Yaoundé: University of Yaoundé, 1989.

Zola, Emile. *Germinal.* Paris: Fasque, 1959.

Teaching about Africa through Literature, Film & Music

Isaac V. Joslin

Introduction: What is Africa, and how can it be taught?

How does one teach about African culture? Is there such a thing as *an* African culture? With competing conceptions of what Africa is – whether the Maghreb is considered separately, what role the American and European Diaspora plays in defining 'Africa', the schism that exists between East and West Africa along cultural, linguistic, and colonial lines – the task of teaching about Africa is intrinsically complex. In addition to these spatial configurations of Africa, one must also take into account the historical palimpsests of Africa: the legacies of great West African empires of the Sahel from the ancient Ghana Empire to medieval Mali and the later Songhai, the Arabo-Islamic influences that accompanied the trans-Saharan trade of goods and slaves, the arrival of Europeans – first as explorers, then as traders, and finally as colonists – followed by the physical and ideological struggles for national independence, the rise of pan-Africanist movements and their evolution within the context of Cold War alignments, and the continuing economic implication of Western powers in African affairs.

The reason why these initial questions are raised here is not because I pretend to propose the answers; I am not certain that any one definitive answer can be reached. Rather, in line with the theoretical framework of my presentation, often raising the questions is a pedagogically effective way of destabilizing supposed certainties and preparing spaces in which one can begin to think critically and independently about Africa, precisely, in terms of its ambiguities, incongruities, and pluralities. This paper proposes that novels, films, and music are particularly effective pedagogical tools that can be implemented in interdisciplinary African Studies classes to engage students in active reflection about Africa, its realities, and its representations.

The Radical Pedagogy of making Strangers

In his article, 'What it means to be a Stranger to Oneself,' Olli-Pekka Moisio argues from a psycho-philosophical perspective that a fundamental step to educating adults about the world, in a way that incites active engagement with real issues, involves what he terms 'a gentle shattering of identities' (Moisio, 490). Moisio postulates that an individual's frame of reference, or the way he or she sees, interprets, and experiences the world is the result of the individuals particular social environment, and as such, the world is a projection, albeit an unconscious one, of the individual's own self-image. Thus, the 'gentle shattering of identities' is a process by which a student's pre-conceived notions about the world are systematically undone through bringing the student to a deeper understanding of himself or herself in its social and ideological conditioning.

Central to Moisio's elaboration of this 'radical pedagogy' is the Hegelian notion that self-consciousness is in fact a dialectical movement of two self-consciousnesses – that of the subject-self and that of the other-object – and this version of consciousness mirrors the Marxist materialist dialectic of the lord-bondsman, which implies a co-dependent relationship between the two parties, actually positing independent self-consciousness in the subaltern role of the bondsman without whom the lord, the socially conditioned self, has no lordship (Moisio, 498-9). Drawing out the implications of this logic for the student of a culture that is different from that of their dominant psychic persona, an intrinsic part of reaching an understanding of the other involves recognizing the other as that consciousness in relation to which one has created one's own identity.[1] This view seems particularly a propos for an application to African Studies, which in Western universities is perhaps the 'discipline' par excellence of the Other.

Moisio's elaboration of radical pedagogy hinges on the connection between the two Freudian concepts of de-realization (the situation in which 'a part of reality is strange to the person having the experience') and depersonalization (the experience of a part of oneself as strange). Moisio does not conflate the two, but argues that, 'when we question some part of or even the whole reality, we are in fact at the same time feeling a central part of our own self as a stranger to ourselves' (Moisio, 501). The self having been formed over time by a continued involvement with a set pattern of experiences that are taken as 'reality', necessarily finds that when this reality is brought into question (that is to say, taken into consideration without the authority accorded by the label of 'reality'), the part of the self that adheres to that no-longer-reality necessarily cedes to an-other self-consciousness, that of a stranger.

It may be helpful to interject here with an example, taken appropriately from African literature. The protagonist in Cheikh Hamidou Kane's *Ambiguous Adventure* (1972), Samba Diallo, experiences a profound existential crisis as he progressively moves away from his traditional home and the Koranic education that was the backbone of his upbringing. Slowly, the reality of this world he had known is brought into question as his Western education and eventual emigration progress, and along with the shattering of his world (which is by no means a gentle one), his sense of self is also shattered, leaving him suspended in what Obioma Nnaemeka calls the 'third term'. Likened to a schizoid sort of alienation, Nnaemeka argues that being present in the third term is in fact a positive and transcendent experience, which for Samba Diallo is the experience of his death and simultaneous re-birth into an unlimited space of possibilities.

Metaphorically, or perhaps symbolically, Samba Diallo's death and rebirth illustrate the ultimate experience of getting outside oneself and thereby becoming a stranger to oneself. This is the very same process that Moisio is advocating as a form of radical pedagogy, though in a not-so-violent or destructive fashion. This approach essentially involves getting students of Africa to see their world as the 'Other' world, and by implication themselves as the 'Other' self; in so doing the students become strangers to themselves and their worldview is then decentered to open up a space that will allow for a meaningful engagement with another world and another self, which would be African in kind. How this is done, I propose here, is through an effective presentation of and engagement with African works of fiction, film and music.

The African novel: an engaging subject
In the introduction to the collective work, *African Novels in the Classroom* (2000), Margaret Jean Hay asserts, 'Perhaps most important ... is the students' ability to relate to fictional characters as human beings, to conceive of African societies as populated by distinct individuals whose behavior, personal concerns, and perceived self-interest can differ widely from one to another' (3). I think that this ability to relate in any context is what draws us as humans to various forms of representation, be they films, novels, short stories or television series. Through close, personal encounters with a, or any number of fictional other(s), one actually loses oneself in the narrative, in the character development, and in the physical, psychological and emotional conflicts that compose a story.

Here it is necessary to make a distinction between losing oneself idly in fictional entertainment and disassociating from oneself and one's typical frame of reference through intentional engagement with entertaining fiction. The former is passive and escapist, whereas the latter is active and focused on obtaining results. This is where the role of the instructor is crucial, and I will elaborate using an example from a recent course.[2]

First of all, students' engagement with and response to a text are largely predetermined by the initial questions that stage the texts. In my course, the question was one of perceptions and hallucinations of selfhood and statehood in sub-Saharan francophone Africa, a question which ultimately aims to examine what constitutes a given 'reality', and what, on the flip side, is dismissed as hallucination, dream, or 'superstition'. With this question in the background, students began reading Jean-Marie Adiaffi's *The Identity Card* (1983) with an eye turned towards the way the characters might perceive themselves and others, as well as the societal structures to which each relates.[3]

The text opens abruptly with a dialogue introducing the ambiguous subject, Mélédouman, whose name means "I have no name' or more precisely, 'they have falsified my name" (Adiaffi, 1), and in an ironic fashion, it is Mélédouman's interlocutor who remains nameless until he identifies himself as a French corporal, second class. Only in the second chapter does the reader find out that the colonial commandant, whose real name is Lapine, has been nicknamed Kakatika, a 'giant monster' (Adiaffi, 7-8). This opening dialogue in which Mélédouman is arrested and brusquely removed from his village by a colonial commandant continues after Mélédouman is imprisoned, successively revealing more about each character's own preconceived notions vis-à-vis the other. Thus, the question of seeing oneself and being seen by/as another is really at the foreground of the text.

The reader is quickly introduced to the racist colonial stereotypes held by the commandant: 'Unfathomable, irrational Africa! Reason will never make head or tail of it' (Adiaffi, 9); 'Blacks were savages, primitive folk with no history, no culture, no civilization,' (Adiaffi, 15). However, the reader is already acutely aware of the subjective bias of these statements as Mélédouman first introduces himself as a prince of the kingdom of Bettié, which is indeed *something*, and he further proves himself, in both conversation and comportment, to be quite adept at presenting eloquent and convincing counter-arguments against French superiority and the 'reality' of the commandant's power (Adiaffi, 27). In a way that is not dissimilar to Ferdinand Oyono's *Houseboy* (1996), the exchange between the commandant and the *indigène* reveals that the ignorant savagery so readily attributed to colonized subjects is in fact more characteristic of the colonial administration in Africa.

What follows is a weeklong journey in which the now-blinded Mélédouman sets out in search of his Identity Card, and though he does not find what the commandant wants – an   objective representation of himself that includes, 'Surname. First name. Date and place of birth. Age. Height. etc. etc.' (Adiaffi, 20) – Mélédouman's quest allows him, and the reader, to uncover truths about his Agni[4] aesthetic, religious, linguistic, historical heritage, as well as his own personal ancestry, which ultimately reaffirm his initial response that 'Only your blood, your family can give you a true identity. Only history can give you an identity. Only time can give you an identity' (Adiaffi, 21, 91). His conversations and reflections that juxtapose Catholicism, French colonial education and territorial expansion with indigenous practices and geographies, succeed in filling in the 'blank darkness' of Africa as postulated by the commandant, and which is also often, unwittingly or not, the view of the preconception of the typical Western university student.

The colonized identity (one whose name has been falsified) is seen on the one hand through the eyes of the commandant for whom identity, and by extension, reality are determined by a set of facts recorded on a piece of paper and imposed from the outside, whereas from Mélédouman's point of view, his identity is a function of a reality that has been denied and negated, and as a result, he must search among the ruins and the fragments of memory 'to the limit of the real and the unreal' to be able to express who he *is* in another way (Adiaffi, 102-3). In a similar fashion, the colonizer's identity is reflected in the mirror of Mélédouman's insightful gaze.[5] This very question of which viewpoint is 'real' and which is not appears as dependent upon the subject's (op)position, implicitly pushes students outside of their own world view to recognize and acknowledge the existence of different co-existing registers of defining one's self and the larger social group to which one claims belonging, thereby gently shattering his/her worldview and corresponding consciousness of self.

African film: visualizing different perspectives
Nicola Ansell (2002) makes a similar case for 'Using films in teaching about Africa,' citing the concept of 'border pedagogy' which, in its essential characteristics, greatly resembles the de-realization and de-personalization characteristic of Moisio's radical pedagogy. Ansell summarizes the aims of border pedagogy as such: 'firstly to unsettle the accepted knowledges promoted through conventional education, and secondly do break down the borders that divide here from there, self from other' (Ansell, 2). Again, the goal is ultimately to bring Africa closer to the student's experiences, so as to avoid reinscribing Africa as yet an-*other* object of study.

Ansell's argument rests on the presupposition that the typical Western student's image of Africa has been constructed based on representations (including movies, not to mention newscasts and infommercials) that depict Africa from an outsider's perspective, and usually in a stereotypical light as a land of famine, poverty, violence and disease. Among the advantages for using film in teaching about Africa, Ansell notes its role in proliferating such images by Western media sources as well as the way it has recently been employed in Africa to construct new images of Africa, address socio-economic, and political issues (as in the notion of Third Cinema), as well as its historical use as a mode of education, manipulation and dissemination of information (e.g. documentary) (Ansell, 3-4). Thus films, especially those produced in Africa by Africans can provide a way for students to *see* Africa as they have seen it before, but from an Other point of view. Again, I will elaborate using examples from the same course mentioned previously.

Unlike many African films of the late 1980s and early 1990s that advocated a kind of pure, 'return to the source' construction of authenticity, Jean-Pierre Bekolo's *Quartier Mozart* (1992) mixes African traditions with African modernity in a provocative way by invoking sorcery as a means to explore gender roles in a popular neighbourhood of Douala.[6] 'Chef du Quartier,' a young girl who appears in a white shirt, tie, and bowler hat (attire that might be a subtle homage to Charlie Chaplin, but which also evokes typically masculine and Western style of dress) is transformed by the sorceress Madame Thékla into a young man who goes by the name 'Mon Type,' so that she can see how things are. The ideal to 'be a woman in a man's body' expressed by Madame Thékla indicates a disconnection between essence and appearance, which is fundamental to Bekolo's cinematic vision, and also provides students with another representation of Africa.[7]

The wedge between reality and representation is driven by Bekolo's innovative, even disruptive editing techniques, including jump-cuts and camera angles that accentuate the exaggerated dramatic qualities of his characters, each of whom introduces him or herself at the beginning of the film by a name or alias (Bon pour un Mort, Chien Méchant, Samedi, etc.). This underscores the theatricality of the production, but also hints at a kind of social performance that is central to African popular culture.[8] The overt emphasis on artifice underscores the role of representation in defining purported 'knowledge' about Africa, and in so doing, the film creates a space in which perception is emphasized, thereby inviting the student/spectator to see and experience *different* images of Africa and Africans.

The film follows a romantic intrigue between the popular and desirable 'Samedi' and 'Mon Type' (the masculine incarnation of 'Chef du Quartier'), which culminates in their encounter at a New Year's Eve Ball portrayed as a montage of snapshots overlain by a soundtrack that mixes African and Western music. This technique mimics the way that significant events are often remembered, in terms of snapshots and soundtracks rather than a complete and linear narrative; and thus it speaks in a universal language to the passionate moments that define the experience of youth. This familiarity opens students' minds to some of the more foreign images presented in the film, such as Madame Thékla's own magical transformation into the man Panka, who upon shaking hands with other men, effectively renders them impotent. Bekolo stages his images of Africa in the context of global modernity, including a reference that Michael Jackson copied from Cameroonian musician, Manu Dibango. The student, therefore, is not only confronted with images of Africa, but also with images of the West from an African perspective, which put him/her in the place of the Other.

Another film that depicts African modernity mixed with traditions in a powerful and ironic fashion is Djibril Diop Mambety's early film, *Touki Bouki* (1973) which, through striking symbolism and stunning imagery, represents Dakar and Senegal in the ambiguous light of their dual inheritance: a rich African cultural heritage and French colonialism and neo-colonialism. This fact is highlighted by the recurring soundtrack of

Josephine Baker's 'Paris' which is playing as the two young lovers, Mory and Anta, dreaming of a better life that awaits them on the other side of the Mediterranean, trek around Dakar in their efforts to steal their passage to Europe. It becomes increasingly evident that 'the little corner of paradise' that, according to the song, Paris represents is in fact not somewhere over there, but right in Dakar as evidenced by Mory's decision, when they finally arrive at the pier, not to depart onboard the 'Ancerville'.

The powerful imagery of the film's opening and closing scenes, which show a young boy riding a cow through the savannah set to the tranquil music of a traditional African flute, contrasts with the overpowering sound of a gasoline engine as Mory rides his motorbike, equipped with the skull of a cow, through the streets of Dakar. The symbolism illustrates on the one hand the violence of colonialism, which laid waste African societies, while on the other indicating the tenacity with which African cultures persist, albeit in skeletal form within the structures of modernity. As such, Mambety's film constitutes a poignant illustration of the seemingly hybrid space of Africa that is forever inhabited by the presence of the colonial Other. These filmmakers take the notion of *cinéma engagé* to another level as they not only deal with concrete social issues, but also reflexively engage questions of representation that have historically constructed the way that much of the world sees Africa. For students of African history, youth culture, or identity politics, the questions put forth in both films invite reflections on the ways in which competing conceptions of the self and other coexist in diverse social milieus, which in turn pushes them to see their own socially constructed selves in light of the chequered pasts that comprise their present state.

African Music: More than mere words
Cultural adaptability in the era of globalization is what defines much of contemporary African literature and cinema; of course, music is no exception. Songs are often used in foreign language classes as a way to engage students with contemporary culture as well as with the language and its poetry. These instructional applications also hold true for African studies courses. Even though the language at times remains opaque, as a number of well-known African musicians, including Youssou N'Dour, Salif Keita, Dobet Gnahoré sing predominantly in Wolof, Bambara, and other indigenous African languages (though sometimes in French), there is still much value in presenting students with the work of these artists whose non-verbal message is loud and clear: the preservation of African musical heritage and its adaptation of modern instrumentations. Of course, in this category, one must also mention the Nigerian pioneer of Afrobeat fusion of traditional African music and jazz, Fela Kuti. With the advent of Youtube, finding and playing music clips and videos is quite easy, and the visual dimension further enhances the students' experience

of the music and dance that is often an integral part of the performance.

There are also a number of contemporary artists who have chosen to share their message in Western languages, including Senegalese R&B artist Akon, Ivorian Reggae artist Alpha Blondy (who sings in French, English, and Bambara), and the popular Malian duo Amadou and Mariam (who also sing in French and Bambara). While the first two artists' musical styles are typically more Western in nature (although R&B / Reggae borrow from African rhythms), Amadou and Mariam do a remarkable job of consistently and seamlessly integrating traditional African instruments and drum beats into their music. There are also a number of noteworthy African musicians that represent a variety of genres, including Senegalese rap group, Positive Black Soul and Ivorian zouglou sensation Magic System.

Often, songs with a particular social or political message can be incorporated into a lesson in a way that considerably enhances the curriculum. For example, in the course that I teach on the conflict in Côte d'Ivoire and its causes, we look back to 1990 when Laurent Gbagbo and his political party (FPI) were instrumental in bringing about official multiparty democracy. Alpha Blondy's 'Multipartisme' (*Masada*, 1992), which opens with a sequence of 'talking drums,' presents a striking indictment of the economic and political situation, pointing the accusatory finger at multiparty politics that are based on ethnic divisions. Another example is that of Ivorian Reggae artist, Tiken Jah Fakoly, whose song 'Quitte le pouvoir' ['leave power'] (*Coup de gueule*, 2004), is a message to any African regime which has outstayed its welcome. Lyrics for these songs and others, often also available in translation, can be found quite easily on the web.

The value of using music in teaching about Africa lies first and foremost, as with cinema, in the students' ability to readily relate to the medium. Furthermore, music is a fundamental element of indigenous African cultures, and it is therefore indispensable to show the ways in which it continues to thrive and evolve in contemporary manifestations. Lastly, music is poetry, and as such, reflects an intrinsic plurality of perspectives and a fluid, changing vitality grounded in the aesthetic rather than rational consciousness, which relates rhythmic and melodic representations of Africa, constituting yet another way of experiencing the rich diversity of Africa and its creation.

Conclusion

Without a doubt, there is a very important and necessary role reserved for historical and analytical texts in teaching about Africa, but what novels, film, and music provide as supplements is an absent pretense to objectivity.[9] As such, these media can lead to an understanding of Africa that stresses the multiplicity of voices and perspectives of subjective experiences in the absence of a single, unifying master narrative. Hence, when properly presented, these kinds of tools prove extremely beneficial for teaching about Africa, as students are confronted with a number of 'other' points of view that *gently* reveal fault lines in their own worldviews and thereby allow gaps to emerge in their self-consciousness, which become the space for an *other* self-consciousness to arise.

This 'radical' stranger-making pedagogy aims to get students to see things differently, or at the very least to see that things can be seen differently. Such an approach can be useful in a variety of courses from History and Political Science to Global Studies and World Literature, carving out space for interdisciplinary exchange between the arts and sciences. Indeed, it is just such an approach that may comprise what, in their article 'Writing the World from an African Metropolis', Achille Mbembe and Sarah Nuttall call 'new *critical pedagogies* ... each of which pairs the subject and the object in novel ways to enliven the relationship between them and to better express life in motion' (252). Though it might be too optimistic to conclude that all students will suddenly begin to see the world from an African perspective, they will nevertheless see an African perspective in a way that engages directly with their own perspective. In so doing, they are pushed outside of the comfort zone of their socially conditioned 'reality' to experience themselves as estranged, as other, which ultimately brings them to a fuller understanding, not only of the other (in this case Africa), but of themselves as well.

NOTES

1 The lord-bondsman dialectic is much like that of the teacher-student. Without the students, the teacher's role is insignificant. Thus, contrary to common intuition, the student is the actual independent agent in the classroom, whose participation in the relationship is the precondition for the teacher's role.
2 A second example to consider, which very much falls in line with this particular type of pedagogical approach is Cameroonian writer Calixthe Beyala's *Your Name Shall be Tanga*. This novel also stages a kind of dialectical, dialogical exegesis of African and Western identity in terms of the relationship between the two women interlocutors, Tanga and Anna-Claude. See Joslin, Isaac, 'Postcolonial Disruptions: Reading the (Feminine) Baroque in Calixthe Beyala's *Tu t'appelleras Tanga.*'
3 One must wonder why the English translation of this celebrated novel is out of print after only one edition.
4 The Agni are a branch of the Akan group of the ancient Ashanti civilization that settled in eastern Côte d'Ivoire.
5 The mirror is also a leitmotif of the book. Mélédouman carries a large mirror with him on his quest, and it is this mirror that ultimately confirms his own identity when his young companion Eba Ya sees Mélédouman's reflection in it (Adiaffi, 89).
6 This claim is, in fact, made outright at the opening of the film.
7 Bekolo's 1996 film, *Aristotle's Plot* endeavors a philosophical engagement with this notion in terms of what 'African Cinema,' and possibly by extension what

Africa itself is or is not, by overtly addressing issues of representation, imitation, the impossibility of authenticity, and so forth.

8   In an interview with Frank Ukadike, Bekolo describes Cameroonian street culture saying, 'It is like a play' (*Questioning African Cinema*, 2002, [237]). Achille Mbembe also discusses this notion in his article, 'Aesthetics of Superfluity,' describing the tension between 'the liquidation of tradition and its substitution by a culture of indifference and restlessness that nourishes self-stylization,' using the term 'superfluity' not only as aesthetic excess that hypnotizes and paralyzes the senses, but also as 'the dialectics of indispensability and expendability of both labor and life, people and things' (374).

9   One student of mine in fact commented that what he enjoyed most about the course was the way in which the fictional element presented issues differently than he had encountered previously in the form of factual articles and analyses of African politics and current events.

WORKS CITED

Adiaffi, Jean-Marie. *The Identity Card*. Trans. Brigitte Katiyo. Harare, Zimbabwe: Zimbabwe Publishing House, 1983.

Ansell, Nicola. 'Using films in teaching about Africa', *Journal of Geography in Higher Education* 26:3 (2002), 355-368.

Beyala, Calixthe. *Your Name Shall be Tanga*. Trans. Marjolijn de Jager. Oxford: Heinemann, 1996.

Hay, Margaret Jean, ed. *African Novels in the Classroom*. Boulder, CO: Lynne Rienner Publishers, 2000.

Joslin, Isaac. 'Postcolonial Disruptions: Reading the (Feminine) Baroque in Calixthe Beyala's *Tu t'appelleras Tanga*,' *Contemporary French and Francophone Studies: Sites* 14:5 (December 2010), 485-93.

Kane, Cheikh Hamidou. *Ambiguous Adventure*. Trans. Katherine Woods. Oxford: Heinemann, 1972.

Mbembe, Achille. 'Aesthetics of Superfluity.' *Public Culture* 16:3 (2004), 373-405.

Mbembe, Achille and Sarah Nuttall. 'Writing the World from an African Metropolis'. *Public Culture* 16:3 (2004), 347-372.

Moisio, Olli-Pekka. 'What it Means to be a Stranger to Oneself', *Educational Philosophy and Theory* 41:5 (2009), 490-506.

Nnaemeka, Obioma. 'Marginality as the Third Term: A reading of Kane's *Ambiguous Adventure*,' *Challenging Hierarchies, Issues and Themes in Colonial and Postcolonial African Literature*, eds. Leonard A. Podis and Yakubu Saaka. New York: Peter Lang, 1998.

Oyono, Ferdinand. *Houseboy*. Trans. John Reed. Oxford: Heinemann, 1966.

Ukadike, Frank. *Questioning African Cinema*. Minneapolis, MN: University of Minnesota Press, 2002.

Teaching African Oral Literature: A Nigerian Perspective

Godini G. Darah

This article attempts a survey of developments in the teaching of African oral literature viewed from the experience of universities and tertiary institutions in Nigeria. The study is not the outcome of a detailed investigation of the situation in all the educational and research institutions where work on oral literature has been done. The focus is on trends and phases of teaching and research, the scholars who influenced them and some of the books and publications that resulted from their efforts. In a narrative of this nature, there are bound to be important names and developments that are either forgotten or not given due recognition. In the study, teaching and research are treated together because, most of the time, the teachers are the ones who are involved in fieldwork and research. The experience gained in teaching oral literature courses guides the approaches to fieldwork and the areas to be investigated. In the Nigerian environment many of the leading teachers and scholars have also produced the books and essential materials used for the course. In the light of this I will give some attention to research works and publications that have shaped the curriculum and pedagogy of the course of African oral literature over the decades.

Interest in the documentation of African verbal arts and oral literatures has a fairly long history. From published records, the initial efforts by Europeans were made in the second half of the nineteenth century. The Europeans involved had political and ideological motives for doing so. The works of Ruth Finnegan (1970, 2010) and Isidore Okpewho (1992) have shown that the early collectors of African folkways were not trained in appreciating the artistic or aesthetic merit of the material they encountered.[1] But whatever the interests of the foreigners were, their efforts have left behind data on ancient forms for literary scholars to evaluate. In Nigeria, one of the earliest documents of this nature is the 1854 book by the German linguist, Sigismund W. Koelle, *African native literature; or, proverbs, tales, fables, and historical fragments in the Kanuri or Bornu language.*

Early in the twentieth century some British colonial officers documented genres of Hausa folklore. Frank Edgar's *Tatsuniyoyi Na Hausa* was issued in three volumes (1911-1913). Neil Skinner translated and edited them as *Hausa Tales and Traditions* (1969). *Hausa Sayings and Folklore* by R. S. Fletcher appeared in 1912 and R. S. Rattray's *Hausa Folklore* in 1913. From the 1930s, written literature in indigenous languages explored the aesthetic features of oral literary genres. This era produced writers who adapted themes and narrative techniques of oral traditions to enrich their works. These writers included Daniel Fagunwa of the Yoruba of the southwest, Abubakar Imam from the Hausa-Fulani section of northern Nigeria, and Pita Nwana whose 1933 novel, *Omenuko*, is regarded as the first in Igbo language. Fagunwa is best known for his *Ogbuju Ode Ninu Igbo Irunmale* (1938) translated into the English by Wole Soyinka as *Forest of a Thousand Daemons* (1968). Imam is celebrated for his *Magana Jari Ce (1937-1939)*, a blend of local and foreign fables. The creative adaptation of oral literary resources continued into the 1950s as evident in the works of writers such as Cyprian Ekwensi and Amos Tutuola.[2]

The creative adaptation of oral forms generated academic interest in them. Adeboye Babalola who became the doyen of oral literature scholarship published translations of Yoruba oral poetry and prose in journals, a process that encouraged him to become a successful teacher and writer later.[3] He completed his Ph. D research on *ijala* hunters' poetry for the University of London in 1964. The thesis provided material for the book, *The Content and Form of Yoruba Ijala* (1966). Babalola blazed a trail for others. Alain Ricard (2004: 34) has remarked that '...Yoruba oral literature is one of the best known on the continent...Yoruba researchers are responsible for much of the best works on oral literature...'

The mid-1960s can be taken as the beginning of the teaching of African oral literature courses in Nigeria. Research work and books by pioneer scholars helped to inaugurate the discipline. Okpewho (1992: 12) has observed that a 'major advance in the study of African oral literature as literature came when native African scholars began to research into the oral traditions of their own people.' In West Africa, J. H. K. Nketia of Ghana was one of the pathfinders in the field. As a musicologist his book, *Funeral Dirges of Akan People* (1955), opened fresh vistas for the appreciation of oral poetry. Also important was *Dahomean Narrative: A Cross-Cultural Analysis* (1958) by Merville J. and Frances S. Herskovits; they investigated narrative traditions of the Fon of former Dahomey from the perspective of social anthropology. There was Jack Berry's *Spoken Art in West Africa* (1961) which surveyed various genres of verbal arts in the region. Bababola's *The Content and Form of Yoruba Ijala* was Nigeria's first major contribution to the emerging discourse. Several other titles from the Oxford Library of African Literature broadened the scope of oral forms in translation, Finnegan's *Oral Literature in Africa* (1970) being the most influential in that decade. These publications provided handy material for the early teachers to design suitable curriculums for the course.

The early phase of the teaching was guided by approaches derived from several academic fields such as folklore, anthropology, history, religion and ethnomusicology, the subjects in which much of the scholarship on Africa was being done at the time. Many of the teachers and researchers were trained in European and American universities and their pedagogy reflected attitudes and biases associated with institutions and the disciplines and theories they were well known for them. To a large extent, the oral materials available in translation determined the content of the course. The number of specialists was small and only a few institutions offered the course. It can be inferred from this background that the curriculum for African oral literature evolved over time and the early set of teachers shaped the scope and direction for its growth as exemplified by the experience in some of the older institutions described below.

The University College, Ibadan, was opened in 1948 as a campus of the University of London but the English Department there did not run African literature courses until the 1960s. The Department of Linguistics and Nigerian Languages which was to play a critical role for Yoruba literature did not become influential until the 1960s under the leadership of Ayo Bamgbose.   Materials on folklore and oral verbal arts were collected and analysed in the Institute of African Studies where J.P. Clark did initial work on the Ijo *Ozidi* epic. Wande Abimbola started his research on Yoruba divination poetry at the Institute. Also at Ibadan, Oyinade Ogunba of the English Department investigated oral resources of drama and theatre in his thesis for the doctoral degree awarded in 1968. Its title was 'Ritual Drama of the Ijebu People: A Study in Indigenous Festivals'. The elements of dance, songs, and audience he examined were to form vital areas of focus for the teaching of oral literature in subsequent years. In Ibadan the course handled by Ogunba was designated 'African Tradition of Oral Literature'; it was compulsory for all students in the second year.

At the University of Lagos a similar process took place in the Department of African Languages and Literatures under the leadership of Adeboye Babalola. The linguistics and oral literary courses were run for programmes in Yoruba, Igbo, and Edo-Benin culture areas. From the 1970s-1990s, Babalola built a team of teachers that included Afolabi Olabimtan, Nnabuenyi Ugonna, Sam Uzochukwu and Tunde Ogunpolu. And of course, J. P. Clark was Head of the Department of English for many years and his influence on the teaching of oral literature and drama was immense. The Centre for Cultural Studies was an additional platform. The oral literature teachers in Lagos later included Felicia Ohwovoriole and Bose Afolayan, both trained in the department.

At the University of Ife, later to become Obafemi Awolowo University, the Department of African Languages and Literatures concentrated on Yoruba linguistics and literature. The teachers of Yoruba oral and written literatures were Wande Abimbola,   Olasope Oyelaran, Akinwunmi Isola,

Bade Ajuwon, Olabiyi Yai (from the Republic of Benin), and Karin Barber of Britain who was doing fieldwork on female oral artists of the *oriki* (panegyric) genre of Yoruba poetry.

Ogunba moved to Ife in 1976 to head the Department of Literature in English and he promoted the teaching of African oral literature. Ropo Sekoni joined the Department from the University of Ilorin. Besides the courses on Yoruba oral literature, students on the Yoruba degree programme took the oral literature courses in the Literature in English Department which were taught by Ogunba, Sekoni, Benedict Ibitokun and myself. Also in the department was Biodun Jeyifo who was doing research on Yoruba popular travelling theatre and his field materials were useful for discourses on orality and performance arts. The approach to the teaching of languages and oral literature at Ibadan, Lagos, and Ife was replicated somewhat at the Universities of Ilorin, Ago-Iwoye, Ado-Ekiti, Adeyemi College of Education, Ondo, and other tertiary academic institutions in south-western Nigeria. At Ilorin the leading authority was Dare Olajubu who did extensive work on masquerade (*egungun*) chants of Yoruba. In all the departments of Yoruba studies in Nigeria, honours essays, theses and dissertations were written and examined in Yoruba language and this policy enhanced the academic integrity of oral literature.

By the mid-1970s a fairly uniform curriculum had been developed with local variations in the institutions. The basic aspects that have featured in the course include general surveys of various oral and traditional genres such as poetry, songs, narratives, the folktale, epics, proverbs, riddles and allied oratorical arts. Other elements are stylistics and literary criticism, translation, and adaptation. Multi-generic forms like epics, festival drama and theatre are sometimes studied from the angle of performance arts. There is emphasis on fieldwork, documentation and preservation as well as training of oral artists and performers. The interface of oral literary aesthetics and written African literatures is examined in detail in postgraduate studies.

The methodology of teaching has also been shaped by the traditions in the disciplines that host the oral literature course in the various institutions. In the English and literature departments, oral literature is sometimes treated from a comparative perspective. The critical canons of written literature are usually applied to the examination of translated oral texts, apparently to demonstrate their status as works of 'literature'. This method has had the unintended effect of undermining the aesthetic autonomy of the oral materials because their mode of creation and articulation differ from that employed in written literature. This shortcoming in criticism is induced by the fact that translations hardly convey the total situation of the resources and nuances that go into the creation and performance of oral forms. The marginal position of oral literature vis-à-vis written literature in the English programmes poses another difficulty. On the average an undergraduate English programme accommodates only a few areas of African oral literature. Students are introduced to the general features of oral genres and forms but their literary characteristics and production mechanics are hardly probed in detail. The fact that the texts are assessed in English translation compounds the situation. In the English-based programmes, advanced courses on theory, literary criticism, field-work, translation and adaptation are taken at the postgraduate level.

In the departments of linguistics and Nigerian languages there is usually more space to treat elements such as folklore background, genre classification, documentation, translation and literary criticism. These aspects are investigated within the corpus of the particular language being studied, not necessarily as part of the larger African heritage. Teachers and students in these departments pay much attention to the collection of field data for transcription and analysis. The data gathered are tested against existing theories and prejudices. In this way the discourse of African oral literature is enlarged and enhanced. The situation of plural languages in Nigeria promotes this approach as teachers and students have limitless reservoirs of original sources to study and document.

From the mid-1970s the gains of fieldwork-based approach to teaching were exemplified by the landmark work done in the English Department in Ibadan under the guidance of Okpewho. His training in European classics, translation, writing and editing showed in the engaging and innovative methods he applied in his teaching and research. He made it mandatory for the students in the oral literature course to undertake fieldwork to obtain material for their final year honours essays. Through this the English Department acquired an archive of recordings from several cultural zones of the country. Even more remarkable was Okpewho's practice of citing the works of his students in his teaching and publications. His relocation to the United States of America in the early 1990s was a loss to the discipline but the English Department has sustained its leading role with the work of teachers like Ademola Dasylva and Olutoyin Jegede.

When the Nigerian Civil War ended in 1970, teachers of Igbo language and literature in eastern Nigeria became visible in the oral literature field. An early fruit of this period was the book, *Poetic Heritage: Igbo Traditional Verse* (1971) edited by Romanus Egudu and Donatus Nwoga, both of the University of Nigeria, Nsukka. The authors say in the blurb of the book that 'Igbo vernacular poetry in both the traditional and current forms has never had the publicity or exposure it merits both by its intrinsic nature as poetry of high quality and as an expression of a people's history, their varied beliefs and their states of mind and emotion. The anthology is a first attempt to fill this regrettable gap.'[4]

The notable teachers of Igbo oral literature were Egudu, Nwoga, F. Chidozie Ogbalu, Nolue Emenanjo, Nnabuenyi Ugonna, and Sam Uzochukwu. The main centres of teaching were the University of Nigeria,

Nsukka, the University of Lagos, Alvan Ikoku College of Education, Owerri, the University of Calabar and of Port Harcourt. In the 1980s, Ernest Emenyonu's initiative of the African Literature Conference series in the University of Calabar helped to broaden the scope for the examination of Igbo oral materials generated from field research. At Nsukka in 1975 and 1976 the Society for Promoting Igbo Language and Culture (*Otu Iwelite Asusu na Omenala Igbo*) sponsored seminars for language teachers. From the papers presented two volumes of essays were edited by F. C. Ogbalu and E. N. Emenanjo with the title *Igbo Language and Culture*, a good resource book for teachers of oral literature. In 1979, Chukwuma Azuonye completed his doctoral degree on Ohafia-Igbo war songs for the University of London and he became active in the Nsukka axis of the 1980s.

Igbo scholars of poetry and theatre also contributed to the discourse and curriculum on oral literature. For example, on the dramatic substance of Igbo myth and ritual, there was a healthy disagreement between M.J.C. Echeruo and Ossie Enekwe. Researchers and teachers of Igbo oral literature and folklore benefited from the exchange. The views of James Amankulor on traditional Igbo theatre and those of Meki Nzewi on music have also improved our appreciation of Igbo oral literature.[5] In the 1980s new scholar-teachers appeared in eastern Nigeria, among them were Afam Ebeogu and Ichie Ezikeojiaku of the Abia State University, Uturu.

In the 1970s the University of Calabar and the University of Port Harcourt introduced courses on oral literature in the English programme. In Port Harcourt, O. L. Okanlawon who was trained in folklore studies in Germany was one of the pioneer teachers. Other oral literature specialists in the department were Nkem Okoh and Helen Chukwuma. J. C. Messenger did fieldwork on the proverbial lore and drama of the Anang and Ibibio and Sam Akpabot published extensively on Efik music and folklore. This background has helped the University of Calabar and the University of Uyo to expand the frontiers of academic investigation into the verbal and performance arts of the language groups in the Cross River basin.

In the English programme at the University of Benin oral literature courses were first handled by Okpure Obuke who did fieldwork on Isoko folklore. Others who have taught the courses include Kola Eke, M. P. Mamudu, and Emmanuel Okwechime. Bridget Inegbeboh who trained in the Department has coordinated oral literature courses at Benson Idahosa University, also in Benin. Mark Ighile, another product of the department teaches oral literature at Redeemers University, Mowe, near Lagos. The teaching of two oral literature courses in the English programme is the common experience in other institutions that have links with the University of Benin. This is the practice at the Ambrose Alli University, Ekpoma, in Edo State and Delta State University, Abraka. At Ekpoma, Benjamin Egede has been the main authority on the subject. I was appointed in 2001 as professor of oral literature and folklore in the Abraka Department of English and Literary Studies. Other teachers of the course are Dumbi Osani and Alex Roy-Omoni. The oral literature courses are taken by majors in English, literature and education, and others from cognate disciplines. There are advanced courses at the postgraduate level. The prospects for oral literature teaching at Abraka improved with the introduction in 2002 of a degree programme in Urhobo language in the Department of Languages and Linguistics.

The number of books published on the folklore of the Hausa early in the twentieth century shows the attraction of the northern Nigeria area to foreign investigators. Literary scholarship on the materials started in Europe and the United States of America but a home-grown tradition did not get established until the 1970s. And the cradle for this was at the Ahmadu Bello University (ABU), Zaria, and its satellite institutions. The Department of English has had a long experience in the study and teaching of popular theatre and folk performances as the publications by Michael Etherton, Andrew Horn and others indicate. Traditions of Hausa folk theatre are also taught at the university's Centre for Nigerian Cultural Studies. From the prism of drama and theatre, Aderemi Bamikunle of English became involved in research and teaching of folklore and oral literature. Abba Aliyu Sani, also of the Department, has carried out extensive research on the nexus between oral and written traditions of literature in northern Nigeria. He is one of the leading teacher-scholars of African oral literature.

In the 1980s, the leading teacher of Hausa oral and written literature in the north of the country was Dandatti Abdulkadir who did his doctoral work on the poetry of Sa'ad Zungur of Bauchi. He was vice-chancellor of Bayero University, Kano, and its Centre for the Study of Nigerian Languages has produced many teachers and translators. One of them, Ibrahim Yaro Yahaya completed his doctorate degree for ABU in 1979 on oral art and socialization process in Hausa. The same year Maikudi Karaye, also of the Centre, received his MA degree from the University of Khartoum on the trickster figure (*gizo*) in Hausa folktales. In the decades of the 1970s and 1980s, the approach to oral literature teaching tended to focus on folklore, popular culture and languages. The trend points to what can be described as the sociology of popular culture and oral literary arts.

On the basis of published works, one of the notable teacher-scholars of Hausa oral literature from the 1980s was Graham Furniss of the University of London. His early fieldwork was focused on the Kano area but his analysis of the output has wider application. His international networks as a founding member and president of the International Society for the Oral Literatures of Africa (ISOLA) have added to the weight of his views on the teaching of Hausa oral literature. With the intervention of new technology of communication the discourse of oral arts has been extended by scholar-teachers such as Dalhatu Muhammed, A. U. Adamu, and Asade Kabir Yusuf to the media of 'home video' and film in Hausa language.

The teaching of oral literature was boosted with the opening of more universities in the north of the country in the 1970s and 1980s in cities such as Jos, Sokoto, and Maiduguri. From the 1980s, more state and private universities and colleges of education have been offering oral literature courses. The universities include those in Abuja, Benue, Katsina, Gombe, Kogi, Niger, Nasarawa, Adamawa, and Taraba. This development has enabled teachers and researchers to undertake studies of languages like Kanuri, Tiv, Idoma, Nupe, Ebira, Berom, Bachama, Gbagyi and others in the 'Middle Belt' states of the country. There are about 300 languages in this section of the country and it promises to be a very rich mine of information on genres and traditions of oral literature. The harvest that awaits fieldworkers is certainly larger than the number of those with the skills and zeal now.

The prospects of publications that will result from intensive studies are indicated by some of the new titles which lay stress on the phenomenon of performance and public display. Examples are Ode Ogede's *Art, Society, and Performance: Igede Praise Poetry* (1997) and Leticia Mbaiver Nyitse's, *Form and Content of Tiv Songs* (2006). Nyitse studied at ABU and teaches oral literature courses at Benue State University, Makurdi. Her book complements publications on Tiv popular theatre and dances by Iyorwuese Hagher, especially his *The Kwagh-hir Theatre: A Metaphor for Resistance* (2003). Nereus Yerima Tadi who teaches oral literature at Gombe State University has demonstrated how the proverbial lore in 28 languages in the state can be harnessed for a variety of pedagogical and communication functions.

The teaching of oral literature was boosted by Nigeria's hosting in 1977 of the Second Festival of Black and African Arts and Culture (FESTAC 77) in Lagos. This was the largest gathering ever of teachers, scholars and artists of peoples of African descent in all continents of the world. The festival featured a colloquium and books on its proceedings recommended increased funding for the teaching and propagation of African folklore, languages and literatures. Two books that appeared in 1981 raised the status of oral literature in the educational system and the public media. One is *Oral Poetry in Nigeria* edited by Uchegbulam Abalogu, Garba Ashiwaju and Regina Amadi-Tsiwala with essays on several subregions. The other book is *Drama and Theatre in Nigeria: A Critical Source Book* edited by Yemi Ogunbiyi. The-500 page book has essays by 28 contributors most of them teachers of theatre and the performance arts in Nigeria. Some other books of the era that promoted teaching are Adebisi Afolabi's *Yoruba Language and Literature* (1982) and Olatunde Olatunji's *Features of Yoruba Oral Poetry* (1984). For teachers and students interested in features common to oral and written traditions of poetry, *The Heritage of African Poetry* edited by Okpewho in 1985 is a useful source book. The samples of translated oral poems represented in the anthology are among the best ever in print and they provide comparative insights into the various genres in the continent. Two other books by Okpewho have been good companions of teachers and students. These are *The Oral Performance in Africa* (1990) and *African Oral Literature: Backgrounds, Character, and Continuity* (1992).

Works on specific genres constantly challenge teachers and students to rethink their theories and methodologies. Some examples deserve mention. Karin Barber's *I Could Speak Until Tomorrow: Oriki, Women, and the Past in a Yoruba Town* (1991) introduces a feminine dimension to a genre usually dominated by male voices. Daniel Ben-Amos's *Sweetwords: Storytelling Events in Benin* (1975) and Ropo Sekoni's *Folk Poetics: A Sociosemiotic Study of Yoruba Trickster Tales* (1991) treat aesthetics of performance techniques in folktales. The poetic riches of Yoruba *Ifa* divination verse are explored in Wande Abimbola's *An Exposition of Ifa Literary Corpus* (1976) and *Ifa Divination Poetry* (1977). The *Ifa* literary discourse has been enriched by new works such as Osamaro Ibie's five-volume *Ifism: The Complete Works of Orunmila* (1986-1993), and Abosede Emmanuel's *Odun Ifa: Ifa Festival* (2000), a 680-page compendium of texts, analysis, and interpretation.

The 'big book bang' of the 1970s was signaled by J. P. Clark's *The Ozidi Saga* of the Ijo of the Niger Delta. The English translation conveys much of the grandeur and delectable nuances of the performance by the bard, Okabou Ojobolo. Clark sees the epic as 'more than a verbal composition ... not so much because it is not written to be read, but because it is the creation of a special type of artist who is a composer-poet-performer, all rolled into one person, working in the multiple mediums of words, music, dance, drama, and ritual.' (2006: ix) These attributes have made *The Ozidi Saga* a treasured work for teachers and students. In the 1960s Clark initiated the academic analysis of the *udje* song-poetry tradition of the Urhobo of the Niger Delta and he describes it as poetry delivered by word of mouth to please the ear and the eyes and move the body. The multi-media features of *udje* have been studied in greater detail in books such as Tanure Ojaide's *Poetry, Performance and Art: Udje Dance Songs of the Urhobo People* (2003) and Darah's *Battles of Songs: Udje Tradition of the Urhobo* (2005). The two books contain about 5000 lines of translated verse which are suitable for teaching and cross-cultural research on oral poetics.

In the fifty years of teaching oral literature in Nigeria several tendencies and approaches have merged to constitute the tradition. There are specialists trained in literary studies who focus on theoretical and aesthetic criticism of the oral forms. These teachers are usually based in the core English and Literature departments. Those in the language departments apply the instruments and methods of linguistics to investigate the oral data and the accuracy of translation is one of their areas of strength. There are some teachers who have entered the field from the academic sites of folklore and cultural studies. The curriculum and pedagogy of the course have benefited from the interplay of the performing arts of drama, theatre, dance, music, and popular culture. Those who operate from these diverse aspects often remind us of the protean nature of oral literature as a multi-bunched discipline of verbal, theatrical, dramatic, audio-visual and performance arts. All the approaches and points of emphasis give special attention to fieldwork documentation, translation and analysis. The Nigerian experience of teaching African oral literature is constantly invigorated by the dynamic flow of professional specializations and methodologies.

A cursory look at many books and publications on African oral literature leaves one with the impression that the pedagogy has been fixated on ancient, archaic and endangered artistic forms. Changes in economic situations, demographic shifts, urbanization and global communication have rendered some of the treasured traditions outmoded. On this account some teachers of African oral literature are finding it increasingly difficult to communicate the values of the forms to generations of students who have not grown up in the rural areas and do not understand the languages in which the literature is created. There is the problem of the passing away of tradition carriers; a problem compounded by the fact that the teaching of the course does not include the production and training of new artists. All those involved in the teaching and documentation of oral literature are hugely mindful of the lament credited to Ahmadou Hampate Ba of Mali that every old person who dies in Africa is like a library destroyed by fire.

Advances in electronic and digital communication have widened the scope for adaptation and transmission of oral literary forms. Many poetic, musical, and dramatic forms are now available in compact discs, videos and global television networks. The composition and dimensions of audiences have been altered and redefined beyond the control of the artists and their patrons. The curriculum of African oral literature studies should be redesigned and expanded to handle these emerging trends in artistic and cultural production and transmission. Finnegan has suggested an approach that can attract scholars in diverse fields of 'comparative literature, film studies, popular culture, music, performance studies' (2010: 27).

Access to books and published materials was an important factor in the teaching of oral literature. Many of the books and journals published abroad were available in local libraries and bookshops. From the mid-1990s it became difficult for teachers, researchers and students to obtain required materials owing to the economic depression that devalued the local currency. Subscription to foreign journals has not been sustained in most institutions and many local ones such as the *Nigeria Magazine* have ceased being published. Many institutions do not have laboratories and studios to support the audio-visual aspects of teaching the course.

Yet Nigeria has made significant contributions to the teaching and documentation of African oral literature. Nigerian teachers and researchers have brought the wealth of the country's experience to the appreciation of the world. Books and essays on Nigeria and translations of various traditions have made an enormous impact on the aesthetics and discourse of African oral literature and written literature as well. As Tanure Ojaide puts it, knowing about 'oral literature helps to understand the subtexts of many modern African literary creations' (2009: 2). With about 500 languages and a population of 150 million, there are vast treasures of oral literature to be mined in Nigeria. There are about 100 academic centres in universities and colleges of education where oral literature features in one form or the other. The future of teaching African oral literature is bright and as Chinua Achebe once observed in respect of artistic energy in Africa, it is morning yet on creation day.

NOTES

1. On the general outlook of early European researchers, see Ruth Finnegan, *Oral Literature in Africa*. Oxford: The Clarendon Press, 1970, pp. 1-47; 'Studying the oral literatures of Africa in the 1960s and today' *Journal des Africanistes*, Societe des Africanistes, Paris, Tome 80 – Fascicule 1–2, 2010, pp. 15–28; and Isidore Okpewho, *African Oral Literature: Backgrounds, Character, and Continuity*. Bloomington and Indianapolis: Indiana University Press, 1992, pp. 3–19

2. Details on the influence of folklore and oral tradition on Tutuola and Ekwensi are available in Bernth Lindfors's *Early West African Writers: Amos Tutuola, Cyprian Ekwensi & Ayi Kwei Armah* (Trenton NJ and Asmara: Africa World Press, Inc. 2010).

3. Vital information on the career of pioneer Yoruba creative writers is contained in 'A Survey of Creative Writing in Yoruba' by Adeboye Babalola and Albert S. Gerard, *Review of National Literatures*, Volume II, Number 2, 1971, pp. 188–205.

4. The book was sponsored under the UNESCO Language Translation Series and published by Nwankwo-Ifejika & Co. (Publishers) Ltd. Enugu, 1971.

5. The essays by Echeruo, Enekwe, Amankulor, and Nzewi are in Yemi Ogunbiyi (ed.) *Drama and Theatre in Nigeria: A Critical Source Book*. Lagos: Nigeria Magazine, 1981.

WORKS CITED

Abalogu, U., G. Ashiwaju, and R. Amadi-Tsiwala (eds.) *Oral Poetry in Nigeria*. Lagos: Nigeria Magazine, 1981.

Abimbola, Wande. *Ifa: An Exposition of Ifa Literary Corpus*. Ibadan: Oxford University Press, 1976.

Abimbola, Wande. *Ifa Divination Poetry*. New York: NOK Publishers Ltd., 1977.

Afolayan, Adebisi (ed.) *Yoruba Language and Literature*. Ife/Lagos: University of Ife Press/University Press, 1982.

Babalola S. Adeboye. *The Content and Form of Yoruba Ijala*. Oxford: Clarendon Press, 1966.

Babalola, Adeboye and Albert S. Gerald, 'A Survey of Creative Writing in Yoruba', *Review of National Literatures*, Volume II, Number 2, 1971, pp. 188 – 205.

Barber, Karin. *I Could Speak Until Tomorrow: Oriki, Women, and the Past in a Yoruba Town*. Washington, DC: Smithsonian Institution Press, 1991.

Ben-Amos, Daniel. *Sweet Words: Storytelling Events in Benin*. Philadelphia: Institute for the Study of Human Issues, 1975.

Clark, J. P. *The Ozidi Saga: Collected and Translated from the Ijo of Okabou Ojobolo*. Lagos and Kiagbodo: Pec Repertory Theatre, 2006.

Darah, G. G. *Battles of Songs: Udje Tradition of the Urhobo*. Lagos: Malthouse Press Limited, 2005.

Edgar, Frank. *Tatsuniyoyi Na Hausa* (Three Vols. 1911 – 1913), translated and edited by Neil Skinner as *Hausa Tales and Traditions*. London: Frank Cass & Co. Ltd. 1969.

Egudu, Romanus and Donatus Nwoga (eds.) *Poetic Heritage: Igbo Traditional Verse*. Enugu: Nwankwo-Ifejika & Co. (Publishers) Ltd. 1971.

Emmanuel, Abosede. *Odun Ifa (Ifa Festival)*. Lagos: West African Book Publishers Limited, 2000.

Fagunwa, D. O. *Ogboju Ode Ninu Igbo Irunmole*. Lagos: CMS Bookshop, 1938; translated into the English by Wole Soyinka as *The Forest of a Thousand Daemons*. London: Thomas Nelson, 1968.

Finnegan, Ruth. *Oral Literature in Africa*. Oxford: Clarendon Press, 1970.

Finnegan, Ruth. 'Studying the oral literatures of Africa in the 1960s and today' *Journal des Africanistes*, Societe des Africanistes, Paris, Tome 80 – Fascicule 1 – 2, 2010, pp. 15–28.

Hagher, Iyorwuese. *The Kwagh-hir Theatre (A Metaphor of Resistance)*. Ibadan: Caltop Publications (Nigeria) Limited, 2003.

Ibie, Osamaro. *Ifism: The Complete Works of Orunmila*, Vol. I – V, 1986 – 1993.

Imam, Abubakar. *Magana Jari Ce*. Zaria: Gaskiya Corporation, 1962.

Lindfors, Bernth. *Early West African Writers: Amos Tutuola, Cyprian Ekwensi & Ayi Kwei Armah*. Trenton NJ and Asmara: Africa World Press, Inc., 2010.

Nwana, Pita. *Omenuko*. London: Longman, 1963.

Nyitse, Leticia Mbaiver. *Form and Content of Tiv Songs*. Makurdi: Aboki Publishers, 2006.

Ogbalu, F. C. and E. N. Emenanjo (eds) *Igbo Language and Culture*, Volume Two. Ibadan: University Press Limited, 1982.

Ogede, Ode. *Art, Society and Performance: Igede Praise Poetry*, Gainesville, FL: University of Florida Press, 1997.

Ogunbiyi, Yemi (ed.) *Drama and Theatre in Nigeria: A Critical Source Book*. Lagos: Nigeria Magazine, 1981.

Ojaide, Tanure. *Poetry, Performance and Art: Udje Dance Songs of the Urhobo People*. Durham: Carolina Academic Press, 2003.

Ojaide, Tanure. *Theorizing African Oral Poetic Performance and Aesthetics: Udje Dance Songs of the Urhobo People*. Trenton NJ and Asmara: Africa World Press, Inc., 2009.

Okpewho, Isidore. *The Heritage of African Poetry: An Anthology of oral and written poetry*. Essex: Longman, 1985.

Okpewho, Isidore (ed.) *The Oral Performance in Africa*. Ibadan: Spectrum Books, 1990.

Okpewho, Isidore. *African Oral Literature: Backgrounds, Character, and Continuity*. Bloomington: Indiana University Press, 1992.

Olatunji, Olatunde. *Features of Yoruba Oral Poetry*. Ibadan: University Press Limited, 1984.

Ricard, Alain. *The Languages & Literatures of Africa: The Sounds of Babel*. Translated from the French by Naomi Morgan. Oxford: James Currey, 2004.

Tadi, Nereus Yerima. 'The ancient in the modern: Contextualizing the African proverb', paper presented at the 8th Conference of the International Society for the Oral Literatures of Africa, Mombasa, Kenya, 15th–20th July, 2010.

```
Teaching African Literature
without Redaction & Hypostasis
```

Chimalum Nwankwo

I

The old question raised by Gayatry Spivak regarding the politics of literature and thought in the metropolis vis-à-vis the rest of the world, still
affects what happens in the classrooms where African Literatures are
being thought. Can the subaltern Speak? Even if the subaltern is allowed
to speak, does anyone care or really listen? This is a cosmo-historical
question encompassing a great spectrum of human and inter-group relationships. I have particularly in mind, the crisis involving the Head of the
African Union. Libya's Gaddafi. The United States of America
commenced its bombing of Libya on the day the African Union's
delegates were supposed to sit down with that mercurial leader and
negotiate his exit from power. The Union, composed of the whole African
continent was ignored. It is in the same manner that those teaching
"strange" subjects like African Literature are ignored when there are suggestions about how to make it worthwhile in the business of international
or trans-national cultural bridge-building.

    In the lives of all nations, there is a spectrum from cosmogenesis to
eschatology which accommodates the entire drama of being and
becoming... Within that spectrum the mind plays out in variegated imaginaries. I have suggested elsewhere that any imaginary which does not fit
into that spectrum in terms of giving meaning to the peoples total
existence is a bastard imaginary. If a belief system floats, if it is ontologi-
cally adventitious, it is useless.To float means that it is there as part of the
perfunctory bric a brac of the culture. It is just there....

    My instruction of African literatures has little faith in psychoanalysis
and African Literatures. The practice is spurious because like all
hermeneutics with universalist pretenses, the whole business is hege-
monically anchored.. If it were to be otherwise, it would make more sense
because the symbols and the inner cartography, the field of internal
dynamics, would have been domesticated ... the proferred template
would be peculiar and particularistic.

124

In other words, the cultural and physical signs which guide any people as they grapple with their various existential questions and problems must have a clear isomorphic relationship with their metaphysical universe.

Not too long ago, at the 2008 Harvard University international conference on Christopher Okigbo, I took issues with a few re-current problems in African critical and creative writing, suggesting embarrassing instances of cultural diffidence. I pooled examples from the older writers to illustrate how certain iconographies and predilections have affected the works of some younger writers. I have also given examples of how what I have called verities of being are reflected in the works of writers from other places, so that you do not begin to imagine that I am into some kind of cultural geo-politics of exclusion. I am insisting that even when we endorse cultural mongrelism it must be a rational cultural mongrelism in which the new cultural animal or the seams of the new bric-a-brac are clear and pragmatic and foundationally enhancing, and not distracting.

My best outside Africa examples are the Japanese Yasunari Kawabata (Thousand Cranes), the Chinese Gao Xinjiang (Soul Mountain Country) and Mo yan(Red Sorghum), and of course the Latin Americans Gabriel Garcia Marquez and Jorge Louis Borges. These are writers who according to the views of one critic suggest that they know how to plunder their cultural past for the benefits of the present.

Permit me to deploy Flora Nwapa's works as the big fulcrum for the rest of this treatise from my classroom experience with African literature, at least in general terms. Here are some of the things coming from Flora Nwapa's works that will endure. But for these things to endure, no redaction must be tolerated in terms of the dynamics of Nwapa's particular world and reality. No other African female writer has clearly and so carefully and so successfully combated patriarchal foundations and institutions like Flora Nwapa. But you have to strive diligently to capture all that for every element of her fiction to be in place for the curious student. The axis of her fictive world is anchored on the Goddess. That anchor secures her feminist thesis beyond that of any other writers. Her work is a perfect example of the triangulated triumph of eco-imagination and ontology and teleology. Her work exists like a natural or unconscious affirmation of what is already there or will remain there progressively, changing only with the consciousnes of Oguta world. Let me explain what I mean. There is Ogbuide, Uhamiri, the queen of Heaven. She is the ultimate foundation of Oguta and the world of Oguta. There is Oguta Lake. There is *Urashi* river. There is a confluence of those two bodies of water. Even though they are antagonistic entities, they exist in complimentarity. That condition nullifies the possibility of male female adversarialism. It also nullifies a singular ascendance and the complex of inequities which arise out of the singularity of ascendance. Man and woman in Oguta depend on those bodies of water for sustenance through fishing and trading. Both fishing and trading are physically unisex occupations. That condition affirms equality or at least sets the condition for equality and the estimation of accomplishments. All contestations draw from the character of that world. So you have a world in which the lens of failure or success are the same. You see that clearly reflected in cultural practices such as the taking of titles. Oguta is probably the only part of Igbo land where a woman could take the title of Ogbuefi or Ogbueshi. That is unthinkable in agrarian Igbo country. Once the playing field for accomplishments and success becomes even, the issue of inferiority and superiority shift from gender to individual. There will be good men and women, lazy men and women, irresponsible men and women, wicked men and women, violent men and women and so forth. Attributes and character traits become human and not gender related. I listened in amusement to a panel which read the difference between Achebe's women and Nwapa's women in terms of historical progression. In other words, Oguta women are different from Umuofia women because of the differences in history and setting. That is an unfortunate distortion of Igbo country and the tendencies of its sub-cultures. In that kind of example, you are not teaching African Literature. You are distorting it through a deliberate or inadvertent but still misleading hypostasis!!! There is also a terrible element of mischievous redaction at play! I am deliberately sounding legalese for reasons that will become evident below.

Essentially what I am saying is that a teacher must have African cultural productions grooved within a trajectory initiating from a particular national cosmo-genesis and stretching through the specific nation's eschatology, drawing in uncompromising accuracy from the foundations of myth , culture, history, private and public memory, in order to arrive at a happy sustained echo of the ontological in the epistemological structures of the nation. A teacher of African literature must see himself or herself as primarily involved in the duty of re-constructiong a world, an unfamiliar world at that. The empire writing back did not end with Bill Ashcroft, Gareth Griffiths, and Helen Tiffin's timely post-colonial intervention, *The Empire Writes Back*. That intervention was appropriately based on the recognition of the fact that there was a damage of the psyche of nations needing recovery. The teacher of African Literature is still engaged in that recovery process. Numerous different situations affirm this.

II

During my days at North Carolina State University in Raleigh on the outreach beats for High Schools and Middle Schools, there were numerous intensely teachable moments for anybody involved in teaching African Literature to foreign students. One particular experience remains in my memory for reasons which indeed have a lot to do with the politics and psychology of culture. After one discussion of *Things Fall Apart* in a Middle School class, a surprisingly irate young African-American pupil virtually leapt up from her seat to challenge my paraphrase of the story with emphasis on the things, the complex architecture of culture, which fell apart in the fictional Igbo country of Umuofia. "Why do you Africans let white people come to Africa and seize all the things which do not belong to them? That's what they do everywhere! And why did you all just let Okonkwo die alone like that without helping him to fight back?" There was shock on the white students' faces in the room of predominantly white students. I put on a blank mask as a teacher commenced shouting at the young lady to shut up. The young lady shot back irrepressibly: "Don't you shut me up! I got to have my say." Security was called in to take her out of the classroom, and "calm" returned.

That day, the sensitivities of that reader-friendly text called *Things Fall Apart* struck me with a special force that I had never imagined or contemplated. I have since then tried to think about the reactions of African students, and of graduate students, and of all kinds of students everywhere before teaching any African Literature text. I can now imagine all kinds of special reactions from different groups with a preparatory reflection on what each group might be expecting in terms of emphasis or elucidation. I have come to the conclusion that context, an old issue in literary criticism must always be part of the drill to make sure that all items of the drama, the great historic agon, between Africa and the West are constantly in pedagogic play and emphasized. I presume nothing at all levels. I create categories and typologies, I define and redefine and explain all items from innocuous language use to the most trivial looking character actions, situating all within the field of context.

Forensics

Elsewhere, I have indicated a preference for the trans-emoted African writing, arguing that there is something more total in the practice of trans-emoting because it is a process or hermeneutic which responds to all things ingrained in cosmology. What we think we are determines how we choose to construct or define and read the world we live in. It is ontology stretching to encompass life and its variation of expedient imaginaries and then of course the eschatology which un-skeins and explains the entire cumulus of human experience. Can we indeed proceed further in this discourse without accepting that in communicating via another language, we are wittingly or unwittingly accepting that some kind of new artifice from a mangled detritus is being re-created. We are part of the team of interventions by Ashcroft, Griffiths and Tiffin who laboured to assert that The Empire Writes Back! The empire will continue writing back in the classroom in pedagogic firmness. We are working with shards or pieces of a bric-a-brac that can no longer be put back together in its pristine or original shape, the kind of attitude which powers the investigations on a crime scene!!! Success becomes a triumphal which is determined by how close the detritus comes to the original state or its mimesis of an existing state.

My premier inclination nowadays has therefore become to see the text forensically. Forensically? Yes! A work of art has become for me a breach of conventional reality. In the case of African literature, the special artifice comes with a new chemistry which must be detangled to reduce or return the composition to a conventional comprehensible reality. My reader or student is part of a jury which must be convinced via my literary legalities that everything is comprehensible; every item fits in the recovered picture. And so, I begin with identifying every single component which must help in the constituting of this new environment. The crime has to be carefully examined and understood. My success will depend on the role which each item plays in affirming the various relationships in view. I know and have realized, by my own practice as a writer, that most writers with any claims to profundity always have that rational positioning of all objects in a text, the breaching artistic field. Interrogations, interventions, mediations, and convincing judgement cannot therefore be without our understanding of the recovered picture in totality.

I proceed with a gambit which grants tentative meaning to the work. This approach always depends on the level of instruction. For undergraduate classes, I demand an ordinary summary or digest, but for graduate classes, I insist on what I call a thematic summary of the work. It is not an ordinary summary in the usual form of digest of actions or events but a summary which takes a position regarding the ultimate aim of the writer. After a general class discussion of the various possible thematic perspectives, deduced from our critical speculations and representations based on consensus, we now make the move which explains the crime, affirming or insisting that the consensus is right or largely right.

Cosmology and Diversity

What kind of world are we looking at? This must be established otherwise we risk applying factional, fractional or universal rubrics in our analysis. We must establish the issue of the world-view or cosmology which houses our text. This work is African literature not solely because it is written by an African but more so because it is written with an African consciousness with a matrix that exudes an African world-view in all facets. In explaining this issue, I am always emphatic about the geographical spread of what

we call Africa. It is not a city or country. It is a continent. I remain mindful
of circumstances in which you meet people from the Western world who
excite this familiar drama. "Where are you from?" Answer: Nigeria. "Do
you know Dr Njuguna. He is from Nairobi or Gabarone or something like
that!"

Africa is a continent with 55 different countries, speaking between
them over three thousand different languages. A country such as Nigeria
has over three hundred different ethnicities speaking that many different
languages , and separated from each other by as much land distance as an
American in Alaska is from an American in Florida. Many of these
languages even when they are spoken in the same country are as different
as French is from Japanese. And yet an African from Nigeria is expected to
know another African from East Africa!!! Trivialize or gloss over this issue
of language, and you find your self in inane and embarrassing quags.

Besides the problem of geographical remove, there is the more complex one of belief systems and the ontological walls between those belief
systems. Contemplate the difference between the Yoruba world-view of
Wole Soyinka and the Igbo world-view of Chinua Achebe. Those two
giants of African literature are from the same country and yet their works
are so different because the cultural matrices are different.

Even when a story is set within a city such as Lagos, Nigeria, one must
recognize the peculiar character or style of life in Lagos because some
times, the setting shifts from urban to rural.The shifts in setting most
often go with shifts in the behaviour of characters, and much of the
cultural cues or markers which determine what happens within the
respective settings spaces. For instance, in Cyprian Ekwensi's *Jagua
Nana* or *Jagua Nana's Daughter*, in Achebe's *Anthills of the Savannah*,
or Flora Nwapa's *One is Enough* or *Never Again* and so forth the drama
and character action change as the various characters move from one part
of the country to the other. When there are such changes, I labour to
explain the cultural implication and the artistic imperatives of the
author. Some times, even within a language group such as Igbo, there are
subcultures compelling their own distinct imperatives. If you miss or
gloss over the implications in character behaviours within such subcultures, you miseducate the students. The very last example here is the differences between riverine Igbo groups like Oguta, Flora Nwapa's home or
chief informational area where she sets most of her novels and that of the
Igbo group of the Idemili (Umuofia) Igbo area where Chinua Achebe sets
the legendary *Things Fall Apart*. The relationship between men and
women are very critical here for any reader who is not Igbo or does not
understand Igbo culture in reasonable depth. If you are teaching the
drama of Wole Soyinka and fail to fully explain very carefully and thoroughly what Ogun, a major deity in the Yoruba pantheon is all about, in
relation to Soyinka's dramaturgy and intriguing character action, you
miss much of what the great dramatist is communicating about Africa

and the world. To understand fully the implication of this recommenda-
tion, try and imagine any teacher anywhere trying to make meaning from
a Shakespearean tragedy without a good and lucid articulation of what
we all know as the Elizabethan world picture, the unavoidable matrix of
Shakespeare's drama.

Realisms: Autochthonous Realism, Magical and Marvellous Realism, Conventional Realism and so forth

From years of looking at African Literature, I have come to the conclusion that in teaching literature, it is also very important to situate the text
written in one of these realisms. When a work comes out as indigenous
in its intensity as in *Things Fall Apart*, or texts such as Wole Soyinka's
plays that have deep roots in the Ogun world, I would classify the text as
based on autochthonous realism, and that calls for a clear perceptive
explanation of what Ogunism, in the case of Soyinka, is all about. Robert
Wren's *Achebe's Magical World* should also serve as reasonable resource
for students who study *Things Fall Apart* in greater detail. And for
Soyinka, the best perception is the kind defined in books by Bascom,
Falola and so forth, where Ogun is clearly placed in the world charged
with the Hegelian impulse or dialectic of destruction and creation and
interminable shaping and re-shaping of the world. That simplifies the
dramaturgy and thematic thrust of plays like *A Dance of the Forests, The
Road, Mad Men and Specialists, the Bacchae* of Euripides. My teaching of
Soyinka will even encompass an argument in one of my papers on
Soyinka in which I suggest that the West may just be enamoured of
Soyinka's work because of what I characterize as a confluence of ontolo-
gies. Ogunism would thus share with Imperialism and Colonialism the
dreadfully flawed notion of the West's endorsement of a human destiny
defined by a so-called Hegelian march of reason through history with its
amoral and nihilistic implications, and share with the slavery concomi-
tant with imperialism, the modus operandi and modus vivendi implicitly justifying the survival of the fittest intellectually, physically, and
materially. I do not fail to point out the ugly political implications there
for Africans and African writers engaged in various activisms and the
psychology and politics of literature. For Soyinka then, as an African
writer, there is an irremediable moral or philosophical contradiction
inherent in his often liberationist or salvationist propensities in the
politics of his art.

I labour to make a clear distinction between magical and marvellous
realism when those strains of realism are in play singly or in conjunction.
There is widespread mis-application of those terms in the academy
world-wide and specifically in studies of Ben Okri's *The Famished Road*
and much of the writings of Amos Tutuola. The magical simply has to

involve actuation of sorts or applied legerdemain. The marvellous does not have to. It is there as part of the expression of a marvellous cosmos. Such distinctions might be considered minute but could become quite significant when peculiar events are being broached for thorough comprehension in a class room.

Understanding the Indigenous Languages of African Writers

Because of the diversity of languages and cultures in the continent, I have in teaching my texts wondered whether I have been able to capture precisely and exactly as possible the ultimate intent of certain African writers especially when African languages, idioms, proverbs, and various ways of reading the African world become woven into the English or foreign languages tapestry of these writers. If we cannot have an authentic African literary expression, as writers agonized over in one of the earlier conferences of the Discipline at Makerere, Uganda, in 1961, I labour extensively to capture what the writers have been trying to do with the colonial language in various ways. There are translations and transliterations in Achebe's deployment of proverbs and Igbo idioms. There is transliteration, with extreme examples in Gabriel Okara's *The Voice*, and there is, of course, what I have referred to as trans-emoting in some of Yvonne Vera's works. It is best to recast the African experience to the foreign reader or some modern African readers who because of geographical location or distancing or birth far away from parental or ancestral norms are unable to speak the language. It is imperative to understand the African language when it is injected into a text by the author. This often happens when circumstances, emotions and feeling or aspects of the culture appear untranslatable. I find it useful to call on several colleagues when I encounter such expressions for clear and careful explanations. It could be quite a disaster to botch a proverb or a phrase in a text when such is there to accentuate meaning or enhance cultural authenticity or local realism. Things as ordinary as tonality in the phonetics of many African languages can cause quite a great deal of confusion if wrongly translated. Here is one disastrous example in a study of Flora Nwapa which could easily have been avoided with a little bit of patience and diligence. In a study of Flora Nwapa, "Applauding a 'dangerous luxury': Flora Nwapa's Womanist Re-interpretation of the Ifo about the 'handsome stranger'" an Igbo poverb is quoted. "ogworo azu ngwere eru ala".[1]

The proffered translation of this is "he who prepared fish for people has always a cheerful face!!!" The correct Igbo translation is "he prepared a lizards-back-cannot-touch-the-ground charm", a proverbial Igbo medicine which prevents a wrestler from being thrown down by opponents.

What student can divine here the translating teacher's error without knowledge of the correct Igbo translation? It is therefore very important to note that even cultural items such as songs which appear in novels like *Things Fall Apart* are not just there for bland lyrical effect but part of the layout of motifs and technical adumbrations of the tragic bole of the text. I do not know that there are many studies of *Things Fall Apart* which have tried to place the tragic song of Ikemefuna in the moral whorl and subtext of the larger tragedy of the inadmissible individualistic and arrogant heroism of Okonkwo.

> Eze elina elina sala
> Eze elina elna sala
> Eze ilikwa ya ikwaba akwa oligholi
> Ebe Danda nechi eze
> Ebe uzuzu nete egwu sala

> King, do not eat, do not eat
> King, do not eat, do not eat *sala*
> King, if you eat you will weep the tears of those who eat
> Where the termites are in coronation
> And the sands dance forever [2]

The child's song emotes the grim inexorable fate of anyone who, like a king, thinks he/she is above the community. What could be more fitting as the foreshadow of Okonkwo's fate, and commentary on the character of a polity where individualism, no matter how heroic, is blighted and checkmated by collective will and the Spirits in favour of communalism?

I would suggest from all of the above that teaching African literature should be approached with the same diligence and level of seriousness which other literatures are approached, especially the attitude which is most common when we periodize other literatures. Context must mean exactly what context means and does for other literatures in terms of a thorough grounding in the world of the text, a seriousness and professionalism which will leave no doubts about the quality of results anticipated or produced for students and scholars in general. Also, it does not matter what paradigms and hermeneutics we arm ourselves with, without domestication of those guiding strategies, the errors in other aspects of African borrowings will be replicated. We cannot afford redaction and hypostasis because we want the African identity recovered or recaptured, and that cannot be without seeking out the ultimate in terms of what the writers mean in their efforts to retell the stories of their various peoples from the furthest reaches of the various cultural empires threatening their identities.

NOTES

1. 'Applauding a "dangerous Luxury": Flora Nwapa's Womanist Re-interpretation of the "handsome stranger"' in Marie Umeh's ed. *Emerging Perspectives on Flora Nwapa: Critical and Theoretical Essays.* New Jersey: Africa World Press. 1998. p. 218.
2. Achebe, Chinua. *Things Fall Apart.* London: Heinemann Educational Books. 1958. p. 42.

Reviews

Edited by James Gibbs

Obi Nwakanma, *Christopher Okigbo, 1930–67: Thirsting for Sunlight*
Woodbridge: James Currey and Ibadan: HEBN, 2010, 304 pp., £55.00
ISBN (hardback): 978-1-84701-013-1

This is an impressive work. The author comments that we so far have few biographies of African writers; and I doubt if there has been another of this thoroughness and care. He has set a high standard for any successors writing the lives of any of their nation's poets or novelists. The book is a labour of love; Dr Nwakanma says that after he first encountered Okigbo's poetry, 'love grew like a mustard-seed'. It is also a work of meticulous scholarship and cautious judgements and reminds one of some of the great biographies published in Britain in the nineteenth century, such as Lockhart's *Life of Scott*, written with intimate knowledge of their subject and a will to help the reader to understand him. Nwakanma has, however, none of the Victorians' ponderousness and none of their inhibitions (just as well, since any life of Okigbo would be dishonest if it didn't mention the poet's voracious sex life).

The work is the story of a *life*, showing influences on Okigbo as an intellectual and a writer, but consciously not a literary critique. It does, however, contain useful pointers to the origin of some of the poems. For instance, the poet's serious passion for music explains the lines:

> I hear sounds, as they say
> A worshipper hears the flutes –
> The music sounds so in the soul
> It can hear nothing else;

and Okigbo's lover, the wife of an American lecturer at Nsukka, was the white queen or white goddess of the poem *The Watermaid*. Because of the clandestine nature of the affair, he writes of covering up her secret with beach sand.

Nwakanma gives occasional expression to his own opinions of Okigbo's poetry. He talks, for instance, of its enchantment and 'its distinct lyrical impetus' and emphasizes the poet's consciousness of himself as a craftsman, framing and polishing his work till 'it glittered like fine crystal'. He also brings out a fact that I for one had not previously realized: Okigbo only began writing poetry comparatively late. His first published poem, *Debtors' Lane,* appeared in *The Horn* (Ibadan) in 1959, when he was 29 years old, after his brief disastrous efforts as a businessman in Lagos. His whole oeuvre was thus produced in less than a decade – and mainly in the seven years before he became embroiled in the Civil War.

The book has several attractions. First, Okigbo's story is that of a person who lived an eventful life and came to a romantic end, which has made him a hero of almost mythic status in modern Nigerian history, particularly among Igbos. He has been compared to Byron, who also died in war, but Byron was a different category of poet – with a fluid and prolific output in contrast to Okigbo's lapidary craftsmanship – and he died fighting someone else's war, whereas Okigbo was, in his mind, fighting for the preservation of his own culture and people. More relevant European comparisons would be with Shelley, who was a similar rebel against the establishment or with Burns, who reminded his compatriots of their own cultural descent, was a flag-carrier for liberty and could also almost match Okigbo's womanizing. These two also died relatively young. Okigbo's life, however, doesn't in truth need referencing by anyone else's. It is an interesting story with a dramatic ending and its context is very specific to a particular era in Nigerian history.

The second attraction of this study is that, while it was completed more than 30 years after Okigbo's death (so that there is a certain distancing perspective on Okigbo's work, life and associates), because the poet died relatively young, many who knew him survived into the time of Nwakanma's research, so he was able to accumulate an extraordinary amount of first-hand testimony to build up his picture. It is unusual to have such a richness of interviews and comments – and also unusual for a researcher to have made such careful and stylish use of the witness material. He has referred to the published commentaries and interviews, such as those by North American and European scholars, but it is the use made of recorded interviews with very many of Okigbo's surviving contemporaries that makes the work stand out. He has voices from almost all phases of the poet's life – family, school-friends, student colleagues, co-workers, fellow-writers – and has been extremely skilful in meshing the evidence from his enquiries into a coherent narrative. He could perhaps have collected one or two inimical witnesses, for instance, the voices of one or two of Okigbo's pupils at Fiditi, where it seems he was not a very successful classroom teacher; but the material he has gathered is pretty comprehensive.

Nwakanma says that his aim was 'placing Okigbo in time and clothing him with spirit'. He has set out to place the poet's life in the historical context of Nigerian politics and African literature. While the literary context is perhaps too vast for him to treat fully, he has provided a splendid and quite dense picture of Nigerian intellectual and political currents during Okigbo's life-time – a third reason for the interest of his work. The poet was a product of a unique time in his country's history: the bridging of colonial rule to the regaining of independence. This is not to detract from the poet's individuality and talents, which Nwakanma shows began to emerge at school.

Early life
Okigbo was born into privilege, as the heir of an Igbo priestly caste, one of the very small minority of his peers to have a secondary and tertiary education. His family background gave him a sense of obligation to the past, while he had older brothers, Lawrence and Pius, who both held high positions in the new Nigerian establishment. Pius, to whom he was closest, obviously had an intellectual influence on his younger sibling, introducing him to a variety of contemporary poets, such as the American Beats. A substantial part of the book (3 out of the 8 chapters) is given to Christopher's early life and his education at first, Umuahia and then, Ibadan. This valuably enables speculation on the development of his personality and attitudes, including his liveliness and flamboyance, which Nwakanma attributes to the death of his mother when he was only five. We are provided with a detailed study of one of the elite boarding schools of late colonial times, modelled on British public schools and largely staffed by British teachers, often men and women of unusual ability. To be a pupil at one of these schools was to be among outstandingly talented peers; many of the Umuahians of the time became movers and shakers in government and politics, business, academe and the arts; and lifelong friendship with such influential men helped to shape Okigbo's career.

There is a remarkable sense of loyalty among former pupils of these establishments, including members of the present-day Umuahia old boys' association, which has launched an appeal to reorganize and recreate the school as they remember it; they recall the collegiality, the commitment of the teachers, the high standards of scholarship and the all-round training. But the schooling could be seen to have made the boys 'men of two worlds'. Nwakanma says: 'In some respects, schooling represented the beginning of Okigbo's conscious uprooting from his primal world', although he also quotes Caleb Olaniyan as saying: 'We were brought up as Nigerians'. The education, of its kind, was undoubtedly good and Okigbo flourished at Umuahia. He was remembered as 'restless, highly intelligent, very friendly, unconventional and very socially involved'. Although he is said to have coasted academically, he appears to have read extremely widely, to have taught himself subjects not on the curriculum and to have shown aptitude at cricket, football, boxing and hockey. He also taught himself to drive from a textbook. The author, in trying to account for Okigbo's womanizing, suggests that the boarding school bred sexual repression, but he tells that while still at school the poet conducted a lengthy intrigue with a young married woman, Felicia.

University career

The translation to University College, Ibadan (UCI) which had only been opened two years before, in 1948, was an extension of the Umuahia experience – an elite community, with high academic standards and a multi-cultural staff, at a time of the 'confluence of cultures' on the cusp of political independence. The student body, being so small, was of above-average talent. The academics included both the distinguished and the eccentric, among the latter being the mathematician, Chike Obi, who founded the Dynamic Party, in which Okigbo involved himself, perhaps from a spirit of mischief, but also with enthusiasm for 'another' Nigeria. At the same time, he had a chance to hurl himself into a vivid and dissipated social life. His close friend, Ben Obumselu, the academic and writer, described their undergraduate period as 'a lost paradise'.

Nwakanma has uncovered some of Okigbo's intellectual influences at the time. He read the Negritude poets, Senghor and Birago Diop and was attracted to the idea of an African aesthetic, although he later emphatically rejected the idea of being an 'African writer', rather than a 'writer'. He was strongly influenced by the poetry of the Congolese, Tshikaya U Tamsi. It should be noted here that Okigbo and other young writers owed a debt to the late Ulli Beier, of the University College's Extra-Mural Department, who translated and published writing from around the African continent.

Okigbo left Ibadan initially without a degree (though he came back later to re-sit), but he already owed it the chance to interact with a wider circle of friends of high ability, including fledgling politicians, such as Bola Ige, later the Governor of Oyo State, and Tunji Otegbeye, founder of the Socialist Workers' Union, and also some of the future military men, in particular Emmanuel Ifeajuna, later at the centre of military insurrection. Arguably, the most important event of his time at UCI was his meeting with Safi Ata, from a noble Igbirra family, with whom he fell deeply in love. Ultimately, against her family's wishes, he married her and although he was constantly unfaithful, she provided him with a stable influence to counteract the frivolous streak in his nature.

The jobs market

The next four chapters are about Okigbo's adult life and various types of employment. A reminder of the different context of the times is the ease with which, after university, even before he had acquired his degree, Okigbo moved in and out of jobs. At the time, employment opportunities for young Nigerian graduates were abundant. In two years, Okigbo could afford to try two jobs in the private sector – with the Nigerian Tobacco Company and UAC, then to give them up for a government post, as PA to Chief Kola Balogun; unfortunately he cocked a snook at authority once too often and lost his place at the heart of politics. In the following four years, he was Vice-Principal of Fiditi Grammar School and then acting University Librarian at the new University of Nigeria, Nsukka, for neither of which posts he had any qualifications! It was, however, in the spirit of that era that young educated people of promise could be given their head.

For someone as volatile and generally negative to authority, it was fortunate for Okigbo, as the ease of finding work gave him the chance to pursue his intellectual and writing interests, which would have been much more difficult in the Nigeria of the twenty-first century, when he might have been left impoverished and ignored. During his lifetime, he even once or twice involved himself in business ventures (including arms dealing during the run-up to the Civil War), but they were not suited to his temperament.

'A Gentleman, Poet and Publisher'

Okigbo's appointment in 1962 to the Cambridge University Press augured the best time of his working life. It took him back to Ibadan, where the University College was going through a golden era; he could reconnect with many of the friends and activities of his undergraduate days; and it was his most productive writing period. Nwakanma characterizes his life then as that of a 'Gentleman, Poet and Publisher' and those of us who knew him at the time would certainly agree. He drove unusual cars, including a low-slung Armstrong-Siddeley (not very suitable for Nigeria's roads), prided himself on selecting fine wines and gathered people into his house for impromptu symposia at all hours.

As Nwakanma explains, one of the meeting places for the intelligentsia of Ibadan at that time was the Mbari Club. It encouraged drama, music, poetry and cultural workshops; Fela Ransome-Kuti (as he was then known) gave one of his first concerts there on his return from Europe and J.P. Clark's *Song of a Goat* was first performed in its courtyard. One of the attractions of its most long-lasting venue was the splendid Lebanese cuisine available upstairs. Okigbo played a very active part in the club and it provided his main cultural recreation, though he took some interest in other institutions: the University College's excellent theatre (Wole Soyinka's haunt), the international film festivals, the literary conferences and workshops of the Extra-Mural Department and the Institute of African Studies. I have a memory of him contributing powerfully and wittily to the discussions at an extra-mural conference on the teaching of literature in Nigeria.

During much of that time, I was in charge of the University College's Extra-Mural Department and so my professional interests ran parallel to those of Okigbo and his contemporary intellectuals; we had a very strong team, some of whose members were also engaged with Mbari. It included Dr Eme Awa, the political scientist, and the writers Obiajunwa Wali, Ezekiel Mphahlele of South Africa and Arthur Drayton of Jamaica. One of our part-time lecturers was Ronald Dathorne, also from the Caribbean (called 'Oscar' in this book). In particular, one of my colleagues was Ulli Beier, whose contribution to the encouragement of new writers and artists is well described by Nwakanma; it used to be exciting when Ulli brought me work by a new writer to see (occasionally it would be a translation for me to polish) or a new artistic project for me to support. Okigbo and other young writers owed Ulli a debt for his energetic help, and as Nwakanma explains, the Extra-Mural Department nurtured many writers' and artists' projects.

Beyond professional connections, Nwakanma mentions that I enjoyed a personal friendship with Okigbo, based on his kindness to me when I had a car accident. The book has many examples of the poet's capacity for kindness and generosity and it was an attractive aspect of his personality. He could, though, be unkind to people he disapproved of or make practical jokes which had an element of thoughtless cruelty, as Nwa-kanma observes. My own experiences of Christopher were good; I think he didn't have many women in his life who were just friends!

Several of the international publishing businesses besides Cambridge employed talented Nigerians and Okigbo seemed to get on well with them. The book says that he was discontented because their employers gave them more scope than Cambridge gave him; and it is true that Aig Higo of Heinemann administered a much larger publishing programme. But I suspect that part of his discontent was self-made; because of his way of life and a certain disorganization in his work, he sometimes let opportunities go and ultimately Cambridge would have found him a maverick employee.

'Biafra and an unmarked grave'

National events then changed the course of his life. Coups and counter-coups (into which Okigbo and some of his friends flung themselves with a rather boyish, not to say amateurish, enthusiasm) led to his feeling that it was not safe for him to remain in Ibadan and in 1966 he went back to the East, arriving a week before his 36th birthday. His biographer says that he had a sense of the profanation of an organic Nigeria, of the kind of pan-national community which he had grown up with in Umuahia and Ibadan. At first, there seems to have been a lively ingathering of Igbo exiles, focused on Nsukka, and Okigbo and Achebe even found time to start a new publishing firm. But in July 1967, after the secession, Okigbo joined the Biafran army, inventing himself as a major in Nzeogwu's guerrilla group, and just over two months later he was dead. He was killed trying to lob a grenade at a tank, a typically quixotic action to end with.

Nwakanma quotes Nkem Nwankwo: 'In some unmarked grave in the

Nsukka bush, the world's worst employee, worst husband and father, finally redeemed himself, was translated like Palinurus to immortality'. This is, however, an unfair obituary. Okigbo was, by any measure a person of extraordinary and varied talents – with wide interests, including his sporting ones, an unusually good memory and avidity for new knowledge – all of which made him always fascinating to talk to. His talent for friendship streams through every chapter of this book. At the same time, he was self-aware enough to recognize some of his own flaws, including his lack of discipline. It is sad that a casualty of the civil war was Okigbo's autobiographical manuscript *Pointed Arches*, which he said was an attempt to trace his creative development. It would have been intriguing to read his judgement on himself as a writer.

In the panorama of Christopher Okigbo's life, his biographer, as said, deserves credit for his skilled description of both the context of Nigeria's independence and its near-disintegration and of the nearer backdrop to poetry of the writer's rumbustious and fairly chaotic life. We are left with astonishment at the crowded adventures of Okigbo's 37 years, and with amazement that he evolved such calm and elegant verse from them. Nwakanma has given us a conspectus of the influences on the poet's writing, ranging from the Yoruba poetry he met in Ibadan and the early West African writers in English to his African contemporaries, met at the 1962 Makerere writers' conference, from classical European authors (Virgil and the Silver Latin writers especially) to the American Beats. He tuned in to the romanticism of Shelley, Keats and Coleridge and to the position of W. B. Yeats as a romantic nationalist in a country emerging from colonialism. He also refined his understanding of language structure and tone by his habit of entertaining himself with translations into Latin.

Okigbo's literary influences were cosmopolitan, and he had chances to travel more widely than many of his friends – in his government job, visiting family (his cousin Bede Okigbo was stationed in Brussels for a while), attending conferences and then on Cambridge University Press business. But, perhaps surprisingly, in his life he was not an internationalist; he was not at home outside Nigeria, in the way that say, Chinua Achebe or Abiola Irele have shown themselves to be. It is hard to imagine that if he had lived, he would have survived in, say, the milieu of a North American university, as many other Nigerian intellectuals have. Rather shy outside his own environment, and consequently apparently arrogant in foreign company, he was through and through a Nigerian, always conscious of his heritage (sending money over many years to keep up the family shrine), living a life-style hard to imagine in more staid environments and in the end dying because of the failure of his vision of a nation.

This reflection comes from reading Nwakanma's study, which also provokes many more. On a minor negative note, there are one or two small errors in spelling of names, (the Sardauna not Sarduana; Tani Solaru, not Solarun) and one could take issue with him on one or two peripheral matters, such as the origins of highlife; but they are insignificant flaws in an exemplary work of scholarship, written with deep affection and without illusion.

Lalage Bown
University of Glasgow

Roger Field, *Alex la Guma: A Literary & Political Biography*
Woodbridge: James Currey, 2010, 258 pp., £50 cloth;
ISBN:978-1-84701-017-9

Anecdotal stories often remain in the mind long after reading a biography and this one is no exception. At the end of the book, the author refers us to a review of the biography La Guma wrote of his father, in which it was asserted that his book was 'at its best when Jimmy's own anecdotes are able to rupture the morality tale of the main narrative.' And the author adds: 'In this work I have tried to achieve something similar for La Guma himself' (231). He certainly has come up with some memorable anecdotes: take the occasion when La Guma and his wife were detained by the security police and only managed to establish that they were in the same prison by singing *La Bohème* and the *Internationale* to one another (124); or the story about the thirteen-year-old Alex, who having read of a speech by Paul Robeson in which he called on writers and artists to fight against fascism in Spain, promptly tried to enlist in the International Brigade (35).

But what of the 'main narrative'? Field, who first became interested in La Guma as a student when he read *A Walk in the Night* and was impressed by the way La Guma handled political issues in his fiction and particularly by the sense of 'an alternative South Africa' the book conveyed, has now written a book which contextualizes La Guma's literary work against the backdrop of South African social and political history from the 1920s to the 1980s. Thus he focuses particularly on the interrelationship of the writer's literary development and the growth of his political consciousness. Convinced from his later reading of such works as *A Soviet Journey* that La Guma 'had grown up in a more complex intellectual, emotional and political environment than most studies had hitherto acknowledged or explored '(3), he examines his life and work in the light of the identity politics of the Coloured community to which he belonged, of the emergence of the liberation struggle to which he was committed, and of the literary and ideological influences which informed his writing.

The book, based on a university thesis which focused on La Guma's time in South Africa (1925-66), has been extended to cover the years of exile he spent in the UK and Cuba and the innumerable journeys he undertook on behalf of the Afro-Asian Writers Association and the ANC. It makes use of a wide range of material, much of it hitherto unfamiliar even to those with an interest in la Guma, and contains abundant excellent illustrations.   This is a project distinguished by assiduous archival research on manuscript sources, and although little private material in the form of diaries and the like has come to light, the author has interviewed many of La Guma's contemporaries. This is a very scholarly biography, which provides illuminating readings both of La Guma's fiction and of his extensive political writings, much of which is not readily accessible. What emerges from all of this is a thoroughly documented, ground-breaking portrait of the writer. I suspect many readers will be as surprised as I was to discover how ready La Guma was to explore different genres and how broad his literary range was, encompassing as it did political journalism, essays on cultural development, travel writing, poetry, radio plays, radio programmes on African writers, and even comic strips (some of which are reproduced in Field's book).

La Guma's varied and often turbulent life provides much of interest for a biographer, and Field does not disappoint. He investigates the author's relationship with his politically active father, describes his life in the decaying Cape Town slum of District Six and his evolving attitude to it ('in it, but not of it', 45), reports his early experiences of racial segregation, traces his early writing talent and accounts for his desire to give voice to the Coloured community which in his view no one had previously portrayed adequately.

There is much necessary detail on the political issues La Guma was concerned about and the campaigns he became involved in (the question of whether Coloured voters should boycott the 1958 elections in which they could only aspire to elect a white representative, for instance). A real strength of Field's account is the moving picture he sketches of a writer harassed by apartheid persecution and yet still struggling to write. Thus, La Guma was one of the 156 accused in the Treason Trial (he thought they constituted 'a marvellous picture of the new South Africa', 77); he endured house arrest, detention without trial, and solitary confinement; he was shot at, and was imprisoned for the possession of banned litera-ture. He wrote the biography of his father while both he and most of his informants were banned. While writing *The Stone Country* his house was frequently raided by the security police, who removed parts of the manu-script, so much so that he constantly had to restart writing (151). Field's book provides a comprehensive account of La Guma's multifarious activ-ities in exile, particularly as ANC representative in Cuba and he discusses his trips to the Soviet Union which resulted in his travelogue, *A Soviet Journey*.

Field's study is full of insight. He shows how La Guma's fiction, journalism and autobiographical writing address similar concerns. He points to the author's interest in popular culture (even American!), as evidenced by his comic strips, which he regards as early demonstrations of his literary abilities. He logs the influences on his writing, highlighting his indebtedness to Steinbeck and Hemingway, and asserting that some of his borrowings amount almost to plagiarism (227). He traces La Guma's concern with Coloured identity in the face of intensifying apartheid legislation and documents his conviction that a true Coloured identity depends on the community becoming part of the liberation struggle together with the ANC. He identifies as a constant theme in the novels the author's preoccupation with the question: 'What enables the individual to convert personal anger or the individual experience of injustice into collective political action?' (217). He gives us a more differentiated view of La Guma's literary practice than hitherto by emphasizing the various ways by which in later years he sought to experiment with literary style and form, for instance in *Time of the Butcherbird*. And he pays due obeisance to La Guma's wife, Blanche, 'never merely the wife of Alex la Guma' (53).

In its incisive account of the interaction of literature and politics in the life of an important South African writer this is an exemplary study.

Geoff Davis
RWTH, Aachen

Ewald Mengel, Michela Borzaga and Karin Orantes (eds), *Trauma, Memory, & Narrative in South Africa: Interviews*
Matatu Amsterdam/ New York: Rodopi, 38 (2010), £50.00
ISBN 9789042031029 and 9042031026

This volume of essays makes an important contribution to Memory Studies as an emergent field of research, while reflecting on how it intersects with psychology and literary studies. It is also unusual insofar as it consists entirely of interviews with South African writers, psychologists, and academics who address the intersections between trauma, memory and narrative from their own perspectives.

What emerges is a sense of how complex and contested definitions and approaches to the three central concepts are. It is precisely the issues related to subjectivity, central to Memory Studies, that makes the interviews an effective approach to exploring these issues from diverse perspectives. The form allows various patterns of interrelationships between personal memory, traumatic experiences and narrative to emerge, without an author/ researcher necessarily formulating coherent findings from the material, as one might expect of a collection of essays or a monograph.

In some ways the patterns of response on shared issues that emerge, in terms of where the interviewees both agree and disagree with one another, are the real contribution of the collection. For example, 'trauma' emerges as a complex and contested concept, often used but hard to define. Many of the interviewees engaged with Archbishop Tutu's assertion at the First Gathering of the Truth Commission that 'Every South African has to some extent or other been traumatized. We are a wounded people' (quoted on pp. 20, 54, 99, 145), to frame the problems of the concept of trauma. Very different kinds of trauma were highlighted, which in turn provokes questions surrounding advocacy: who may speak for whom, and the ethics and effects of 'writing' and reading trauma. It was also very clear that neither the dominant psychiatric definition of Post Traumatic Syndrome (According to the American Psychiatric Association, cited pp. x, 106, 127-136), nor classic treatments, like Eye Movement Desensitization and Reprocessing Therapy (pp. 93, 178) are necessarily universally appropriate. Much of this has to do with the fact that 'trauma' has tended to be viewed as an event, as opposed to an ongoing lived experience; also that socio-economic realities often preclude people from being removed from the traumatic situation. These nuanced psychological insights by experts make accessible subject-specific issues and concepts, thus extending typical humanities approaches to these issues in meaningful ways. Indeed, the research most often cited throughout the interviews is the cross-disciplinary collaborative work of Pumla Gobodo-Madikizela, associate professor of psychology, and Chris Van Der Merwe whose research focus is Afrikaans and Dutch literature.

From a literary perspective, both via writers and academics, the collection asks very important questions about the role and efficacy of reading and writing in a post-traumatic situation: contrasting 'taking an ache and holding it to the light and seeing it for what it is', as a form of healing through letting go, with the potential danger of 'retraumatization'. They also reflect in interesting ways on the efficacy of the TRC, suggesting unanimously on its significant contribution to South Africa while expressing particular reservations that continue to be explored in and through various creative media.

A fascinating issue that emerges almost implicitly through the collection is the distinction between autobiography and memoire, particularly in terms of the levels of fiction involved and how this relates to Zoe Wicomb's concept of 'misremembering'; and the consequent role these forms have in the reconstruction of history in contemporary South Africa. This suggests that issues of narrative are important beyond issues of genre. They extend to how narrative is being used to construct and challenge formulations of national identity in terms of personal and collective experience, and what constitutes 'trauma'. This is particularly significant if one considers South Africa's history and current levels of violence.

Although I found all the interviews contributed in particular ways to understanding how trauma, memory and narrative intersect and inform one another in the South African context, three interviews in particular struck me. The first was the interview with Miriam Fredericks and her team at the Trauma Centre in Cape Town, which outlines the scope of contemporary violence and trauma dealt with in the centre, which is relatively under-resourced. Twenty personnel, of whom fourteen are psychologists or social workers, do individual and communal counselling, networking, organize commemorative events and engage with media outreach projects to raise the profile of issues of torture in South Africa, while doing advocacy work closely related to Human Rights related organizations. They have a Political Violence Programme, a Children and Violence Programme, a Trauma Response Programme and they work with local refugees. Don Foster, a professor of psychology, extends Miriam Fredericks' reflections on the effect of internalizing trauma and torture for an individual, and by implication the society as a whole (99, 109). His use of a theatre paradigm to reframe roles and relationships between perpetrators and victims of violence; for example, by approaching them as 'protagonists', Foster nuances binary positions of blame and power and the complexities of the relationship between South Africa's past and present. It explores ideas in psychological terms, while using literary metaphor, raising similar questions to those raised by Mark Saunders in *Complicity* (2002), and J.F. Coetzee in *Waiting for the Barbarians* (1980). The argument is provocative, and perhaps for this reason it may offer an effective way of revisiting the past that allows South Africans to break the cycles of violence and blame. It also reemphasises the importance of grounded interdisciplinary paradigms and research.

The third interview that struck me was with Helen Moffett. Throughout South Africa gender issues have been subsumed into race discourses as exemplified in the statement, 'rape continues to be rewritten as stories about race, rather than gender' (229). In this interview Moffett demonstrates how certain traumas are specifically gendered and emphasizes that 'Gender is a matter of life and death'. She clearly and at times painfully traces how male violence relates to constructions of masculinity and how these are directly related to the past, to 'institutionalised, almost structurally shaped patriarchal violence' (228). She offers deconstructions of models that prevent change and indicates radically new ways of approaching gendered violence.

This collection does not convey ideas via a coherent, theorized paradigm, but offers multiple and sometimes contradictory ways of engaging with complex concepts. The sum is greater than its parts, and we as readers must actively engage with the positions, views, and provocations expressed. Appropriately, I would argue, for surely action is central to agency and change. My only disappointment with the collection was that the editors did not position themselves in relation to the material, nor are they included in the biographical notes. This seemed completely contrary to the spirit of this collection which foregrounds perspective and subjectivity. Surely it was they who chose the interviewees, formulated the questions, and edited the responses; thus defining the emergent narratives? Perhaps it was a modest gesture towards not wanting to appropriate ...? Nevertheless, their stories are crucial to our understanding of the biography of this project and so their absence is significant.

Yvette Hutchison
Department of Theatre and Performance Studies, University of Warwick

Malika Ndlovu, *Invisible Earthquake: A woman's journal through stillbirth*
Athlone, SA: Modjaji Books, 2009, 88 pp., R 130.00,
ISBN 978-0-9802729-3-2
Fiona Zerbst, *Oleander*
Athlone, SA: Modjaji Books, 2009, 56 pp., R 120.00,
ISBN 978-0-9802729-7-0

When I was asked to write a book review, having a choice of books, I went by the back cover blurbs and decided to take the above two collections of personal writing together, admittedly without knowing anything about the authors, because, according to the descriptions, they shared the theme of pain. Searching for information on the authors to fill in my gaps, I found out that they are well known in South Africa. Both of them were personally present and represented by their publisher and their latest books at the Cape Town Book Fair in June 2009. In fact, one photograph on-line shows them sitting right next to each other during a reading at the fair. Their publisher, Modjaji Books, founded in 2007, a small but growing South African enterprise that 'wants to fill a gap by providing an independent outlet for serious writing by [Southern African] women "that takes itself – and its readers – seriously,"' markets its books through Blue Weaver in Africa and through the African Books Collective in England.

Malika Ndlovu, 'born in 1971 in Durban, ... poet, playwright, performing artist and arts project manager' believes in the 'therapeutic power of the arts'. *Invisible Earthquake*, devoted to 'Iman Bonigwe Ndlovu, Born and buried 3rd January 2003,' documents a woman's lasting pain about the stillbirth of her daughter and third child. The first and longest part of this volume is a mix of poems and diary entries subdivided into the years

2003, 2004, 2005 and 2006, followed by a postscript from 2009. The second part is accompanying material related to stillbirth. In a conversation, two maternity hospital social workers, Muriel Johnstone and Zubeida Bassadien, share their experiences about and with women who had been through the experience of stillbirth. Also accompanying the volume are medical facts about stillbirth by 'a specialist obstetrician' (72), Sue Fawcus, a resource section with references to books, websites and support groups, two pages of acknowledgements and a brief author's bio. The creative and the factual part complement each other and speak to the issue that though the pain a woman experiences is utterly individual, it is at the same time known to millions of other women. By voicing the pain and trauma caused by her loss, Ndlovu shatters the silence and breaks a strong taboo. In doing so, she reduces the likelihood that women mourning for children that did not have a chance to live will endure glib remarks, such as the unfeeling advice to 'just get over it', 'give it another try' or 'get pregnant again', or suggestions that it is the woman's fault, suggestions that create or enforce feelings of guilt.

In this moving testimony the reader becomes witness to six years of pain, the attempts to keep the memory of the baby alive, to cope with depression, to lead a life after the internal, thus invisible earthquake, to become happy again without forgetting. The stillbirth in the seventh month of pregnancy '... tore my world in two / as quakes do' (19). There is the internal damage, the rubble, death, the before and the after. In Ndlovu's entry from May 1st in 2003, the pain is still so present that speaking to others about it seems impossible: 'I'm navigating in and out / Of mental combat / Trying to figure / Exactly what station I've pulled into, / How to answer that simple question / How are you? // An invisible earthquake dulls my senses. / I hear myself speak / From a distance, / See their eyes blur in sympathy / Feel their embraces...' (27). At the end of the month another poem attests explicitly to Ndlovu's belief in the healing power of writing: 'I write to keep you alive / I write to resist killing myself / ... / I write to cleanse myself, / ... / I write to remember the instants of acceptance, / A stream of light entering my imprisoned heart. / I write to liberate us both, / ... / I write to relive the moments / That were only yours and mine, / ... I write to engrave you in memory / ... / I write to run from forgetting, / ... / I write to calm my fear / Of losing all trace of you. / I write to draw myself out / Of the dark well of doubt. / I write to come to peace / with you being there / And my not yet knowing where // I write to keep myself / And you, my baby, / Alive' (29-31). The same poem also expresses solidarity with women who share her fate and the wish to give them a voice: ' I write for women who know this / Unbearable / Unspeakable / Irreversible separation. / The desperation of clinging to sand / On that lonely shore, / Where the ocean simply / Continues to rise and fall, / Persistently pushing and pulling us into a new day / Even when we thought we'd run out of ways / To live with this absence' (29-30). Three years later, in December 2005, Ndlovu is able to write that she is on the way to recovery: 'As this third year closes I sense a fundamental shift / A crack in my shell / Where light has begun streaming in / Warming my new skin / ... / I have developed a comfort in the dark / A hunger for the dawn / In my bones I know / I have grown wings' (53). Keeping the memory alive also implies keeping it alive for her son who was two at the time of the stillbirth. Just two and a half weeks after that entry Ndlovu observes how her son has been speaking of his sister as a firm presence:

> Your beautifully articulate almost-five-year-old brother has been talking about you more than usual lately. He tells everyone that he has—not had—a sister, but she died and, depending on his audience goes off into elaborate explanations of how you fell from the sky. His latest drawings of our family include you larger than anyone else. (56)

While the author envies her son for his innocent relationship to his dead sister, one can also interpret the conversation with his mother as more ambivalent, less positive, and therefore as a sign for potential danger to the son's emotional health. When he says, 'I love you, Mummy and I am your alive son, my heart never stopped yet, hey?' (56), one can hear the fear that he may die, too, and the care for his wounded but slowly healing mother. This reversal, if only temporary, of the parent-child roles may be too heavy a burden for a five-year-old who appears to take on the trauma of his mother. The personal narrative ends with Ndlovu's post script from January 2009 in which she tells us about her healing progress:

> Just over a year after Iman Bonigwe's passing I gave birth to Kwezi Michio. ... His was an unplanned-far-too-soon-but-then-again-perhaps-perfectly-timed pregnancy. ... His physical presence is for me inextricably connected to her physical absence. His growth and milestones hardly ever pass without my thoughts lingering, even for a second, on how it would be if she were here or remembering the depths of sorrow that he lifted me from when he entered our lives. (64)

Ndlovu thus confirms her doctor's observation of thirty years of practice that 'a new birth cannot cancel out the previous death of a baby. It cannot replace the loss, but it can serve to provide a new source of great joy' (80).

Fiona Zerbst's fourth volume of poetry, *Oleander*, concerns itself mainly with pain, personal pain, for example caused by divorce, but also with pain caused by history and nature. She is quoted online as saying about herself that she 'specialise[s] in writing about economics, finance, health, fitness, psychology, travel, books, people. Style varies, from humorous and academic to factual and investigative.' Sometimes, these are mixed in one poem. According to The African Books Collective's blurb, Zerbst was born in 1969 in Cape Town, 'has lived in Johannesburg and Cape Town and is currently based in Rustenburg in the North-West Province. She spent six months in Ukraine and Russia and has visited Argentina,

Vietnam, Cambodia, Malaysia and Egypt. She works as a freelance writer
.... Previous volumes of poetry include *Parting Shots* (1991), *The Small
Zone* (1995) and *Time and Again* (2002).' In addition, Zerbst has worked
as an editor and is a lover of crime fiction, 'especially the really "dark"
stuff.' Her poem 'Crime fiction,' is included in *Oleander* (28).

Zerbst's travel experience finds expression in many of *Oleander's*
thirty-six poems and has inspired historical references, from the very first
one that also contains the oleander that gave the volume its title,
'Remembering S-21, Cambodia' (8-9) to 'Relics' (11) which is a reminis-
cence on her travel to Egypt, to 'Impermanence' (13) that features the
tsunami in South-East Asia in December 2004, 'Laguna Frias, Patagonia'
(42) and 'On a lake in Patagonia' (44-5), 'In Saigon' (53), possibly 'Light'
(54) which could be about a mosque in Egypt, to the one directly
following, 'Besides the Nile' (55-56). Some poems contrast beauty with
devastation, such as the already mentioned oleander in a former
Cambodian school-yard-turned-prison where torture took place. Others
are painful in their keen observation of common events, like moths
burning in the light (which can also be read as a political poem about the
situation of Blacks and 'Coloureds' in pre-1994 South Africa), or a dog
dying after having been hit by a car.

The most poignant poems are those that deal with personal relationships and divorce, and feature a marked. resistance to giving in to the pain
(12) and glimmers of hope for a new life after the break-up. 'Beach-town
revisited' (21) reads as the attempt to mend a relationship at a place sym-
bolising former happiness:

'...As you turn, / I sense the blur of me begin to burn, // to want you back, intol-
erably, trying / to think of some excuse, to sing some words... / A seagull
perching on a ring of rocks / that waits until the wind permits a take-off... / I
haven't any answers, but I offer / the best of me, aware of what's at stake. // It
wasn't right for six years, but I'm calling / your name, the only name; and watch
waves break.'

In 'The dying fish' (27) the fish is stranded on 'flattened sand,' '... a
paragon of need. / As patient as a leper, // watched and rotting.' Written in
the first person singular, the poem stands also for a person feeling
stranded, helpless and hopeless. Resistance to this feeling of being
stranded or helpless are represented in 'Learning to box' (12) in which we
read '[a]fter a year, I started throwing / punches in my sleep. / ... / Fear
and sweat / were far away, as they / are when finally / it is just me // with
my footwork, / natural speed, the will to live.'

In 'Comfort' (14) divorce is directly addressed, the worst pain is over,
the rain-clouds open, and she describes how suicidal feelings are
overcome:

'...the river had no need of me / but let me add my few tears to the stream. / ... /
... In the year of our divorce, / winter's rains were uttered with a guttural /
grating in the drains, below my window, // where I sat and waited for my life. /

Now the rain's magnanimous. Its wet hands / pat the sullen earth; its tiny drops / are pinpricks of my former pain. And wet salt / shivering on leaves is like an omen: // what was once alive; what can be again...'

One poem in this collection, 'Legacy—after Frida Kahlo' (46-47), in a way, summarizes the ambivalence of pain, by taking the Mexican painter Frida Kahlo (1907-1954) whose life and work have become, as she suggests, the symbol of suffering, resistance, strength and beauty as its subject:

'Her legacy of nails in flesh, / Tears of pomegranate: // A broken column / Painted as herself. // ... // As she paints, / She dreams with her hands. // As we watch, / A butterfly sticks // To coils of her hair. / That flat plate of brow // Is a golden canvas / to feast from.'

Both Malika Ndlovu and Fiona Zerbst leave their mark with their ability to apply razor-sharp language which is at times hard to digest to express and share their pain and open up paths for a healing process. Their books are no easy read but definitely worthwhile.

Pia Thielmann
Independent scholar and poet

Helen Moffett. *Strange Fruit*
Athlone: Modjaji Books CC, 2009, 56 pp. R. 120
ISBN 978-0-9802729-6-3

Poetry that rewrites a personal history is always of interest, particularly in the current post-colonial era so deeply affected by global neo-liberal interests. And so out of a diaspora of forms and traces feasts rooted in such uncertain ground, the likes of Helen Moffett's *Strange Fruit* grows. Each poem in this collection reminds the reader that beyond all form, beyond the metaphor, the metonymy, the simile, the hyperbole, there lies a living person grappling with politics at many levels. It may therefore not come as a surprise that the poems in this collection speak of chaos, despair, ecstasy, and faith, not hope.

Helen Moffett's *Strange Fruit* is a rewriting of the poet's experience as a woman, poet, and academic working in South Africa. In a strong personal voice, Moffett's uncertainties and ambivalence about her lot as a woman and plight as a professional artist reach beyond her cultural boundaries as she comes to interpret who women see themselves as, are seen as, and may be glimpsed in different ways as in *the body politic*.

This *body politic* is at the core of her work as it encompasses the corporeal, artistic, academic and broader political couched in a doubting voice that builds on the strength of its own doubting through auto-biographical references to issues of identity and belonging. In turn, this doubting voice builds on the speaker's vivid representation of her lived experiences as woman, daughter, lover, wife, mother, but most of all as writer.

So, all references to African and other fruits should be taken with a grain of salt. In 'Cape Town', Moffett's doubting, though at times shrill voice builds on a vivid representation of Cape Town — not its actual, but rather ideological, weather. In a similar vein, all of her descriptions go beyond the confessional mode often associated with lyrical poetry grounded in autobiography and for that matter beyond merely decorating a post-colonial *locale*. In fact some of the poems in this collection defy the very idea of belonging (see 'Fade' and 'Relativity' in particular). On the other hand, some of the poems are so grounded in the female experience that they might detract from the collection's political stance.

Moffett is interested in the past and present as politicized second-hand text; an experience known to the reader as a purely translated experience that needs to be *engaged* with. This means that the authentic and original meaning of the post-colonial predicament from the female experience can only be communicated to the reader as a purely translated experience through myths, hand-me-down tales that are appropriated through identi-fication or confrontation, and simply via the circumstances of telling as conveyed in 'The disa that found us':

> We were struck not blind,
> but dumb, both pointing
> at the manifestation alongside the
> crumbling ridges of the jeep track:
> arising out of an unpromising bush...
>
> Very British Brian
> had never seen a disa before; and I,
> the botanist's daughter, had failed
> to look closely enough, note the
> lobes of green like tonsils in the throat
> striped with white, clean as toothpaste.

Moffett displays here strong technical control of complex thoughts and affects, while unrolling a fluid series of images, rich with significance beyond their materiality. This is both a subtle and a punchy achievement, for the speaker is able to convey the slippages of time and imagination, memory and presence, need and desire, as pivotal to the object and purpose of her art at this point in time.

Dominique Hecq
Swinburne University of Technology

Conteh-Morgan, John & Assiba d'Almeida, Irene, *The Original Explosion That Created Worlds: Essays on Werewere Liking's Art and Writings*
Amsterdam/New York: Rodopi, 2010, 363 p., $87.30,
ISBN: 978-90-420-2971-2/ E-Book ISBN: 970-90-420-2972-9

Living and working in Africa, Werewere Liking has made a tremendous impact on the Francophone world. This collection of essays demonstrates that Liking's works have struck an optimistic tone for nation-building in Africa.

Part I buttresses Liking's vision and practice of art and literature; highlighting her ability to dig into African cultures for personal and collective transformation. Michelle Mielly reads Liking's works as revolutionary instruments, and the Kiyi-Mbock Village as a new social organization in which women are not simple productive and reproductive objects, but agents, in possession of the word at the origin of creation.

Notwithstanding, argues Juliana Nfah-Abbenyi, the word has lost its power in decadent contemporary Africa. As a result, an exceptional approach is required; the kind that only the masked agent performs. Nfah-Abbenyi aptly captures Liking's iconoclastic use of the masked agent to eradicate the symbolic 'Tsetses'. This agent, the new female artist, a 'deity' inspired by powerful women of the past, lives and works for the well-being of all. Peter Hawkins concurs and emphasizes that as an artist, Liking is a savvy blender of genres. Hawkins highlights the multicultural dimension of Liking's works as well her aspiration to use 'total art', or 'multimedia' in a transformative way.

Yvette Balana likewise believes that critics and readers need a multicultural background to decode Liking's works. She majestically debunks the idea that Liking is hermetic. Linguistic mannerisms, constant recourse to neologisms, such as 'Misovire', can be easily understood when the reader is familiar with the myths and legends that are fundamental to Liking's world vision.

Part II highlights Liking's audacious use of fictions to transgress and subvert negative social orders. When selfish and greedy people – or 'Tsetses' – take over the public arena, someone must take up the engaged function of a female M'Bock whose words are meant to heal. Eloise Brière ranks Liking among writers who advocate 'Rubenism', the ideological approach of the Cameroonian nationalist Ruben Um Nyobe. Um Nyobe, together with Soundiata Keita, is a model for new and promising fighters, such as Ruben, who feed on century-old stories, as well as recent ones, to forge a new society free from decaying traits. From this perspective, the artist is a transgressor who breaks silence and brings hidden truth to the collective tribunal.

Odile Caseneuve sets out to portray Liking as artistic entrepreneur and founder of the Kiyi-Mbock Village, the symbol of the new Pan-Africa. In providing groups of young and old artists with education, a tool for survival and nation building, Liking and her two sisters become heads of a thriving village. Liking's audacity consists in pitting brave women against failed father figures in order to erase the 'rifts in the psyche'.

Hélène Tissière's geographical and aesthetic approach raises a number of questions including: What links can be made between a fourteenth century Mandingo myth and a nineteenth century Bassa myth? And, how, and with what purpose, does Liking connect painting and writing, orality and writing, poetry and the novel in a single volume? Tissière's reading helps us to see things as circular and multidimensional, rather than linear. The past is embedded in the present in order to better shape the future, and, since cultures function empathically not exclusively, the local no longer feels threatened by the global.

Part III unveils unknown dramatic texts and highlights Liking's sources of inspiration. Judith Miller captures the role of marginalized women, especially the liquid 'heroines' such as Ngoh Hikweng Manyim in the Bassa myth of origin. These women strive to bring back the light without which society sinks into acts of self-destruction. The quest for rebirth posits Ngo Hikweng Manyim as the textual representation of the Kiyi-Mbock Village women who endeavour to save Africa's youth. It is in this sense that Liking's writing is also a meta-discourse, a self-critical discourse. This was the late John Conteh-Morgan's position on Liking's work, and he drew on examples of theatre in Francophone Africa to better emphasise Liking's inventive, innovative, creative and self-reflexive forms.

Part IV centres on Liking's poetic work, and argues that every body of work is a constant reworking of pre-existing ideas. From that perspective, argues Joseph Mwantuali, *On ne raisonne pas le venin* embodies what Liking has attempted to do, be it theatre, art work, or novel. Mwantuali echoes other critics to contend that the poet is a 'goddess' whose targets are the young and female 'others', the pillars of the new social order. Like Senouwou Dabla, he believes Liking is among those post-colonial intellectuals who believe that nation building requires a return to roots. Dabla goes on to talk of a 'Transgeneric' movement and to link Liking to the Negritude Movement.

Part V centres on the difficult task of translating Liking's work, a 'synesthetic experience' which consists in mixing '... [the] poem with other linguistic stuff...' Liking's translators are poets engaged in the process of 'Speaking pictures, Seeing Words'. Marjolyn de Jager writes about her years of painstakingly rendering Liking's works into English. Following this, Jeanne Digome digs into the Bassa culture to better grasp the ritualistic and, thus, the poetic dimension of a work that has successfully tapped into rituals and legends.

In Part VI Irene D'Almeida Assiba produces a superb investigative piece that buttresses Liking's ascension to Pan-African and international fame. A well informed critic, Assiba contends that Liking has provoked many kinds of analysis, and aptly shows how journalists in Africa, Japan and France, as well as renowned university critics, have presented a body of work that has had an impact on many lives. None of them has successfully aligned Liking with existing forms. Consequently critics, like the 'transgeneric' artist, have to be innovative and inventive.

Gilbert Doho,
Department of French and Francophone Studies,
Case Western Reserve University, Cleveland, Ohio

Erratum in ALT 28: Film in African Literature Today

The publishers regret that an error was made during the typesetting of the article by Greg Thomas entitled 'Haile Gerima's "Message to the Grassroots": Hearing Malcolm X in Amharic – or Harvest 3000 Years'. The first paragraph of the Conclusion on p. 66 should have appeared not as part of Greg Thomas's own text,but as an epigraph quoting Françoise Pfaff, 'Haile Gerima (1946–) Ethiopia', *Twenty-Five Black African Filmmakers* (1988: 139).